ULTIMATE GUIDE TO

D0689306

Masonry
AND Concrete

CREATIVE HOMEOWNER

ULTIMATE GUIDE TO

Masonry AND Concrete

DESIGN · BUILD · MAINTAIN

CREATIVE HOMEOWNER®, Upper Saddle River, New Jersey

Senior Editor: Mike McClintock
Assistant Editors: Daniel Lane, Sharon Ranftle
Editorial Assistants: Evan Lambert, Jennifer Ramcke
Copy Editor: Neil Soderstrom
Photo Researchers: Robyn Poplasky, Sharon Ranftle
Technical Consultants: Dennis W. Graber,
    National Concrete Masonry Institute &
    Gregg Borschelt, Brick Institute of America
Indexer: Schroeder Indexing Services

Senior Designer: Glee Barre
Illustrations: Robert LaPointe, Glee Barre
Cover Design: David Geer

Front Cover Photography: John Parsekian/CH
Back Cover Photography: *top* Jerry Pavia; *others* John Parsekian/CH
Principal Photographer: John Parsekian
Photo Assistants: Frank Krumrie, Dan Lane
Photography Models: Frank Krumrie, Dan Lane,
Sharon Ranftle, Jennifer Ramcke

Creative Homeowner
VP/Publisher: Brian Toolan
VP/Editorial Director: Timothy O. Bakke
Production Manager: Kimberly H. Vivas
Art Director: David Geer
Managing Editor: Fran J. Donegan

Printed in the United States of America

Current Printing (last digit)
10 9 8 7 6 5 4

Ultimate Guide to Masonry and Concrete: Design, Build, Maintain
Second Edition
First published as *Masonry: Design, Build, Maintain*
Library of Congress Control Number: 2005908263
ISBN-10: 1-58011-298-6
ISBN-13: 978-1-58011-298-7

CREATIVE HOMEOWNER®
A Division of Federal Marketing Corp.
24 Park Way, Upper Saddle River, NJ 07458
www.creativehomeowner.com

Safety

Although the methods in this book have been reviewed for safety, it is not possible to overstate the importance of using the safest methods you can. What follows are reminders—some do's and don'ts of work safety—to use along with your common sense.

- Always use caution, care, and good judgment when following the procedures described in this book.
- Always be sure that the electrical setup is safe, that no circuit is overloaded, and that all power tools and outlets are properly grounded. Do not use power tools in wet locations.
- Always read container labels on paints, solvents, and other products; provide ventilation; and observe all other warnings.
- Always read the manufacturer's instructions for using a tool, especially the warnings.
- Use hold-downs and push sticks whenever possible when working on a table saw. Avoid working short pieces if you can.
- Always remove the key from any drill chuck (portable or press) before starting the drill.
- Always pay deliberate attention to how a tool works so that you can avoid being injured.
- Always know the limitations of your tools. Do not try to force them to do what they were not designed to do.
- Always check that any adjustment is locked before proceeding. For example, always check the rip fence on a table saw or the bevel adjustment on a portable saw before starting work.
- Always clamp small pieces to a bench or other work surface when using a power tool.

- Always wear the appropriate rubber gloves or work gloves when handling chemicals, moving or stacking lumber, working with concrete, or doing heavy construction.
- Always wear a disposable face mask when you create dust by sawing or sanding. Use a special filtering respirator when working with toxic substances and solvents.
- Always wear eye protection, especially when using power tools or striking metal on metal or concrete; a chip can fly off, for example, when chiseling concrete.
- Never work while wearing loose clothing, open cuffs, or jewelry; tie back long hair.
- Always be aware that there is seldom enough time for your body's reflexes to save you from injury from a power tool in a dangerous situation; everything happens too fast. Be alert!
- Always keep your hands away from the business ends of blades, cutters, and bits.
- Always hold a circular saw firmly, usually with both hands.
- Always use a drill with an auxiliary handle to control the torque when using large-size bits.
- Always check your local building codes when planning new construction. The codes are intended to protect public safety and should be observed to the letter.

- Never work with power tools when you are tired or when under the influence of alcohol or drugs.
- Never cut tiny pieces of wood, vinyl, metal, or pipe using a power saw. When you need a smaller piece, saw it from a securely clamped longer piece.
- Never change a saw blade or a drill or router bit unless the power cord is unplugged. Do not depend on the switch being off. You might accidentally hit it.
- Never work in insufficient lighting.
- Never work with dull tools. Have them sharpened, or learn how to sharpen them yourself.
- Never use a power tool on a workpiece—large or small—that is not firmly supported.
- Never saw a workpiece that spans a large distance between horses without close support on each side of the cut; the piece can bend, closing on and jamming the blade, causing saw kickback.
- When sawing, never support a workpiece from underneath with your leg or any other part of your body.
- Never carry sharp or pointed tools or materials, such as utility knives, awls, or chisels, in your pocket. If you want to conveniently carry any of these tools, use a special-purpose tool belt that has leather pockets and holders.

Contents

Introduction

Masonry is a crucial part of most houses, literally holding them up with concrete footings and foundations made of concrete or block. These traditional and durable materials take so many forms that they are used in countless locations, both inside and outside the house.

In *Ultimate Guide to Masonry and Concrete: Design, Build, Maintain*, you'll find information on the full range of masonry materials and applications, including basic concrete, block, brick, stone, glass block, stucco, ceramic tile, and more. You'll learn not only the basics but also how to complete some challenging installations. There's even a section on maintenance and repairs for each type of masonry.

You'll find the information you need about tools and techniques to work with masonry. There are also dozens of step-by-step photo sequences and cutaway drawings that show how to build the most popular projects. The extensive selection covers several types of patios and walkways, landings and steps, retaining walls, fireplace hearths, and many more—all built the right way and built to last.

GUIDE TO SKILL LEVEL

Easy, even for beginners.

Challenging. *Can be done by beginners who have the patience and willingness to learn.*

Difficult. *Can be done by experienced do-it-yourselfers who have mastered basic construction skills and have the tools and time for the job.*

Design

Pattern and Texture
Color and Tone
Size and Scale
Site Orientation
Slopes and Drainage
Curves and Corners
Walk and Drive Options
Design Galleries

CHAPTER 1

Pattern and Texture

No matter what masonry material you're working with, and regardless of the color, you can create a great variety of patterns and textures. This is possible because most masonry used in walks, walls, patios, and other structures is built of small modular units. You can set them with butt joints or end to end, or in a random pattern, repeating pattern, or combination.

Even plain concrete can be imprinted or stamped with metal forms before the mix hardens to create a grid or simulated stone pattern.

With brick, there are many types of repeating patterns, such as herringbone and running bond. But complex patterns with bricks set at odd angles to each other can create a lot of cutting and trimming work along the edges. Things become even more complicated if the pattern is bounded by a curve.

You can keep the installation work simple and still vary the overall texture of a basic pattern by combining it with different types of borders and insets. Borders can be quite complex and can bound not only the overall structure but also intermediate areas. They can also enclose a small centerpiece with a special design.

Modern tile is available in groups of complementary patterns and colors.

Different units form unique walls.

Embedded stones form a uniquely patterned walkway.

Insets of different shapes create a focal point in a plan.

Different patterns can define areas of a walk or patio.

Varying the size of a material creates intricate textures.

Color and Tone

Masonry materials offer a wide color pallet that you can use with other building materials inside and outside the house. Most materials come in a variety of earth tones, but you can also lay stone that is pitch black and brick that is bright red.

Even concrete can be spiffed up simply by adding colorant to the mix. You can do the same thing with mortar to create joints in block, stone, brick, or tile that blend in with the surrounding masonry or create a contrasting pattern.

Many masonry projects offer several ways to create either a unified or contrasting effect. For a flagstone patio, you can select all the stone from one color batch, which will provide subtle differences from one piece to another but a unified appearance overall. Another option is to select from different color batches, such as dark reds, deep blues, and light grays, and build in a random pattern of striking color combinations.

Similarly, on brick projects you can use one color batch and create focal points and contrasts by laying the bricks in complementary patterns. You can also use contrasting colors in a standard herringbone pattern or use one color for the main field and another for the border.

Many masonry materials are available with subtle color shadings that you can use to enhance a pattern.

Tile with graduated color shadings forms a color mosiac.

Subtle shadings of tile can unify complex spaces.

Combinations of colors form unusual countertops.

Bold colors contrast with typical earth tones of stucco.

Size and Scale

Well-designed walks, patios, drives, and garden walls can unify outdoor and indoor areas. They can also create valuable new outdoor living spaces that are extensions of your home. Your site is unique, presenting its own set of challenges and opportunities, but a few rules of thumb can guide your design.

One is to unify your landscape by using elements that share a common trait or characteristic. A wall, for instance, might have a contrasting pattern of large and small blocks but with a repeating sequence of size and color.

Another principle is to create a focal point for the plan. You can do this with the overall scheme, creating a layout that converges on a central feature. And you can carry the idea through in construction details—for instance, by laying a large or specially shaped stone in the center of a wall or walkway.

Generally, a symmetrical layout tends to appear more formal, while an asymmetrical plan is more casual. But you can mix the two approaches at various points in your overall design. For example, you might build a formal patio centered on the house wall with a symmetrical border of bricks but integrate the centerpiece into a system of informal, curvilinear walks and planting areas.

Masonry laid in a grid can unify turning walkways.

Combine large and small grids to create borders and focal points in a field of tile.

Changing the scale of materials within a masonry wall can create a one-of-a-kind structure.

Variations on a basic grid pattern can unify areas finished with different types of materials.

Site Orientation

The position of a walk, drive, patio, or garden wall is most often determined by the location of existing building and property lines. But if you have options, such as building a patio on one side of the house rather than another, it pays to consider site orientation.

Take into account the natural breezes on the site and the path of the sun overhead. You may want to build a patio or a garden wall to take advantage of maximum solar exposure or maximum shade—or something in between.

Generally identify your site's desirable views and natural features, such as trees, rocks, and streams, and plan your new walk, patio, or drive to enhance these features. You can unify your landscape by selecting and using materials that are similar in size, shape, color, material, texture, or detail, and create cohesiveness among the various elements of the site.

Masonry walls can create flat yards on sloped sites.

SUN AND SHADE

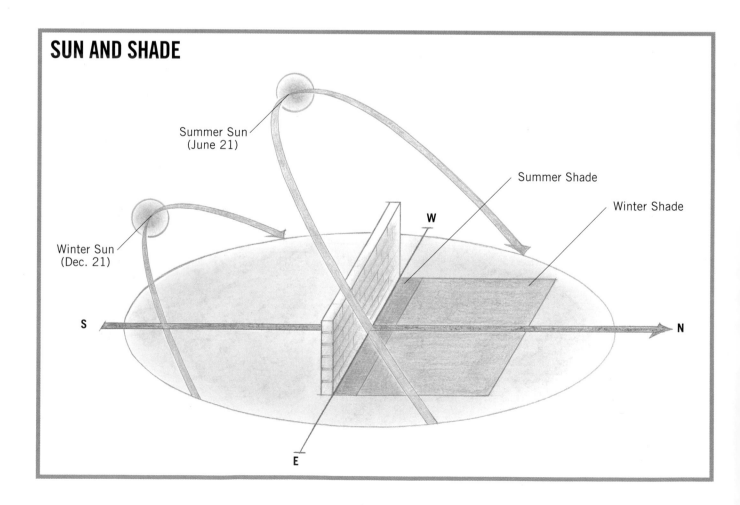

Summer Sun
(June 21)

Summer Shade

Winter Shade

W

Winter Sun
(Dec. 21)

S

N

E

Brick walls built with an open-pattern bond form boundaries while creating an airy appearance.

WIND AND VENTILATION

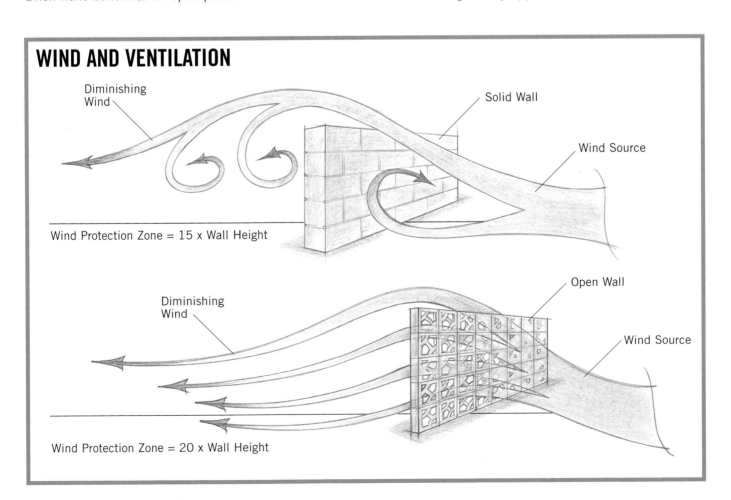

Diminishing Wind

Solid Wall

Wind Source

Wind Protection Zone = 15 x Wall Height

Diminishing Wind

Open Wall

Wind Source

Wind Protection Zone = 20 x Wall Height

Slopes and Drainage

When designing a site plan, you can make drawings for walks, drives, patios, and landscaping features on a sheet of paper. But two-dimensional plans may not account for drainage channels, berms, and other ups and downs in the yard.

Although many flat structures, such as patios, are built with a slight slope to promote drainage, they are basically level. If you want to install them on sloping ground, you need to plan for steps and more than one level. But there's no reason why drives and walks made of masonry materials can't travel along a reasonable slope.

One approach is to terrace a slope by cutting away sections and using the dirt to fill adjacent areas. This work is most economical if you plan ahead to remove roughly the same amount of dirt as you need for fill. But this will create distinct level changes and will require steps.

On installations of bricks, pavers, gravel, stone, and concrete, you can form a gradual and consistent slope by raking out the supporting dirt. On many jobs you can use a base layer of gravel or sand to establish a grade.

In all cases it's important to thoroughly compact supporting layers of fill as well as the dirt at the bottom of the excavation. This helps to reduce shifting and reduces maintenance and repair time later on.

Slabs of stone form steps that follow a natural slope.

PLANNING SLOPES

To establish a slope, divide the vertical distance (rise) by the horizontal distance (run). A slope that drops 2 feet in 25 feet has an 8-percent incline. You can measure rise and run with a tape measure, using a stake, string, and a line level to lay out and check dimensions over large areas. Minimal slopes on patios, drives, and walks are enough to encourage drainage.

Area	Recommended Slope	
	Maximum	Minimum
Patio	2%	1%
Walk	5%	0.5%
Yard	4%	0.5%
Bank	25%*	—

* For a bank planted with grass, a slope of up to 50% is acceptable if the bank has unmowed ground cover.

Stone walls can provide a flat terrace for yards or gardens against a sloping drive or walk.

Random-pattern stone patios can be joined with steps.

Stepped capstones will level a sloping wall.

DRAINAGE FOR DRIVES

I f there is no natural slope to your driveway, you need to create one to provide adequate drainage. Good drainage also reduces maintenance. Three possibilities (shown at right, front to back) include a cross-slope to one side drain, a concave shape channeling water to one or more center drains, and (one of the most common layouts) a centerline crown that sheds water to two side drains.

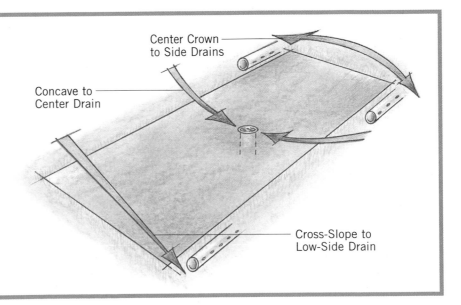

Center Crown to Side Drains

Concave to Center Drain

Cross-Slope to Low-Side Drain

Curves and Corners

It's easy to design curves on paper with a compass. But it's important to try some of your design options outside, so you can discover how they translate to full scale.

To see how different curved corners will look on an otherwise straight wall or walk, for instance, you can lay out various arcs using a stake and string. By moving the stake position close to the corner and shortening the string you can swing a tighter arc. Moving the stake farther away and lengthening the string creates a more gently sweeping arc. Once you decide on a shape, mark it for excavation by holding a can of spray paint or a chalk box at the end of the string as you swing the arc.

Irregular curves, with a decreasing radius, for example, and serpentine shapes with multiple curves are difficult to lay out precisely. That's why most people use a length of garden hose to approximate the shapes. A hose is easy to move around as you can try different combinations. It also holds its shape for marking.

Bear in mind that basic curves are relatively easy to lay out but considerably more difficult to build than straight shapes with square corners.

You can build graceful, serpentine brick walls, or define areas with a zigzag pattern of poured concrete.

FORMING A CURVED WALK

First, use a garden hose to lay out curves and several sticks the same length to maintain the width.

Second, mark the final curves with spray paint or chalk just outside the hoses as an excavation guide.

Third, dig up the sod and 2 to 3 in. of soil between the marked lines, and rake the ground free of stones.

Fourth, dig a trench along the edges with a shovel, deep enough so that the edging will rise above grade.

Fifth, set edging blocks into the trenches to contain the surface material and prevent erosion.

Sixth, spread gravel or other finishing material onto the walk in layers, and tamp each layer firmly.

Walk and Drive Options

Although asphalt is used more than other materials for driveways, there are appealing masonry options, including concrete, pavers, brick, and stone. The choice is important because driveways (and main entry walks) are a prominent feature of today's houses. Driveways are often the main access route into the house.

Most walks are narrow enough for you to install flat without having to worry about runoff. But driveways, which are wider, generally need a slope to encourage runoff. A slight rise along the center of a wide drive won't be noticeable.

As a general guide, size the main part of a driveway between 10 and 12 feet wide for a one-car garage, and 16 to 24 feet wide for a two-car garage. (If the drive will form part of a walkway, add another 2 feet.) An apron that tapers out to meet the street makes it easier to back your car in or out. Extra parking that doesn't obstruct normal activities is extremely useful; allow 12 feet per vehicle for cars, more for trucks and RVs.

Take the time to lay out drives and walks with stakes and string (or a hose for curves) so that you can visualize the overall space and see how your vehicles fit before starting work.

You can lay basic end-to-end patterns of mortarless brick to make a transition from narrow walks to wide patios.

CHAPTER 1 **Design**

WALKWAY AND DRIVEWAY MATERIALS

Concrete slabs make strong, long-lasting driveways as long as the ground underneath is relatively stable and the pour is reinforced with welded wire. This rugged material can appear slightly commercial looking, however. You can improve its appearance by imprinting patterns (a process called pattern stamping) on the surface before the mix hardens. One drawback: light-colored concrete will show oil stains.

Concrete pavers have the same durability as poured concrete; some blocks can withstand up to 2,000 psi of pressure, which is more than enough for driveways. The many seams are weak links in the system. Pavers come in a wide range of colors and styles, so it is easy to complement the look of your home. While fairly simple to lay yourself, professional installations cost more than poured concrete.

Stone and brick can make durable drives, but they're not a good choice for steep driveways; they tend to get slippery when wet and collect ice in cold climates. In terms of installation, if you're looking to save money, brick that is set on a sand bed costs less than brick with mortared joints set on a concrete slab. Stones can be set in a mortar or sand bed, or placed directly on well-compacted ground.

Gallery Design

Every successful masonry project begins with a well-planned design. Depending on which materials you choose to complete your project, different considerations must be taken to ensure a job's success. Incorporating these decisions into your initial design will save time and money.

Wall tiles (opposite) are thinner and lighter than floor tiles, but are available in the same variety of styles.

Coursed rubble walls (above) require more meticulous planning and construction than random rubble.

Firebrick (above right) is prepared to resist heat better than regular brick.

For every design goal, there's a face brick to match. This brick walkway (right) achieves a weathered look.

A glass-block partition creates privacy in a bathroom (far right).

Stucco's versatility is its greatest advantage: it can complement almost any landscape (below).

Tools

Layout

Excavation

Mixing

Cutting

Setting and Finishing

Hand

Power

CHAPTER **2**

Basic and Specialty Tools

Most masonry work requires basic tools that many people have around the house, as well as a handful of more-specialized items, such as trowels and floats for finishing. The collection shown in this chapter will serve for most projects, but you can check the tool list with each project to find out exactly what you'll need.

A basic collection of rulers, squares, and levels will allow you to lay out a typical masonry project. You'll also need a chalk-line box to snap guidelines and a set of mason's blocks and string, used mainly on block construction. Each wooden block hooks onto the corner of a block, and the string stretches tightly between them to serve as a guide for all of the blocks in the course.

To square up measurements and draw cut lines for form boards, use a combination square. A framing square is handy for checking corners. But you can also use some measuring tricks to check your forms and layouts. One trick is to compare diagonals. If your patio forms are square, then the diagonals will be equal.

Another trick is to use the proportions of a 3-4-5 triangle. If one leg is 3 feet long, another is 4 feet long, and the hypotenuse is 5 feet long, the angle between the two legs will be exactly 90 degrees. The 3-4-5 system works at any scale, so you can square up a small set of steps in inches and a large patio in yards.

Some of the tools used on larger projects are definitely not DIY items. One example: a vibrating tamper used for compacting soil, gravel, and sand. If you're building slabs, patios, or walkways, it's wise to rent one.

The same holds true for excavating jobs where you need to dig a lot of holes. The basic posthole digger will do for one or two holes, but for larger jobs consider renting a power auger, either a one- or two-person model.

CHAPTER 2 Tools

Layout Tools

MEASURING TAPE

4' LEVEL

MASON'S BLOCKS AND STRING

FRAMING SQUARE

CHALK-LINE BOX

Excavation Tools

SPADE

SHOVEL

RAKE

PICK

POSTHOLE DIGGER

VIBRATING TAMPER

TAMPER

WRECKING BAR

AUGER

Mixing, Cutting, Setting, and Finishing Tools

A clean wheelbarrow makes a handy mixer for mortar and modest amounts of concrete. And unlike a mixing tub or trough, it's easy to move around the work site. But bear in mind that a 40-pound bag of concrete makes only about ⅓ cubic foot, and a 60-pound bag only about ½ cubic foot. On larger jobs you can rent a portable mixer to save time. On big projects such as a patio slab, order concrete from a ready-mix company.

To cut block, brick, and other masonry, the most important tools are a short-handled 2-lb. hammer and a cold chisel or brick set. These hardened tools are tough enough to score and break block and brick. Another option is to use a standard circular saw with a special masonry cutting blade. This operation produces a lot of debris, so wear a dust mask in addition to the standard protection of gloves and safety glasses.

The most commonly used tool is a mason's trowel, available in several sizes that you can match to the scale of your project. Use it for placing mortar, forming furrows, buttering the ends of block and brick, and trimming mortar flush at joints. You'll also need one or more floats to handle surfacing work, and special trowels to cut control joints and form edges on concrete jobs.

Mixing Tools

WHEELBARROW

HOE AND TROUGH

SPINNER MIXER

PORTABLE MIXER

Cutting Tools

CIRCULAR SAW AND MASONRY BLADE

2-LB. HAMMER AND CHISEL

MASON'S HAMMER

BRICK SET

Setting and Finishing Tools

METAL FLOAT

DARBY WOOD FLOAT

BULL FLOAT

TROWEL

EDGER

JOINTER

GROUT BAG
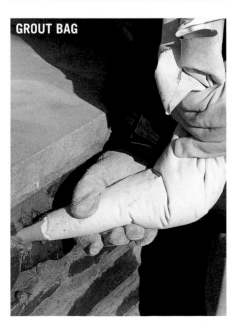

STRIKING TOOL

RUBBER MALLET

CHAPTER 2 **Tools**

General Hand Tools

HAMMER

HANDSAW

HACKSAW

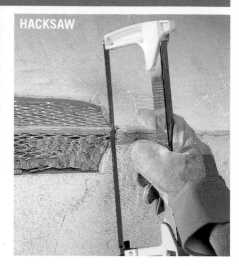

PLIERS

WIRE BRUSH

WHISK BROOM

CROW BAR

HOSE WITH ADJUSTABLE NOZZLE

CAULKING GUN

CHAPTER 2 Tools

Power Tools

RECIPROCATING SAW

DRILL

SABER SAW

GRINDER

Safety Tools

RUBBER GLOVES

WORK GLOVES

SAFETY GLASSES

KNEEPADS

SAFETY GOGGLES

RESPIRATOR

PARTICLE MASK

EAR PROTECTORS

Concr

Mixes

Forming

Reinforcing

Pouring

Finishing and Curing

Maintenance and Repair

CHAPTER 3

Mixes

Concrete is a mixture of portland cement, gravel or crushed stone (aggregate), sand, and water. Easily worked when wet, concrete hardens into one of the strongest of all building materials. The workability and strength of concrete depend on the quality of the ingredients, their relative proportions, and how they are mixed.

The key ingredient is portland cement, a mixture of lime, iron, silica, and alumina that is fired in a kiln and ground to a fine powder. When mixed with water, cement forms a paste that binds sand and gravel into concrete. There are five basic types of portland cement, each intended for a different type of construction. Type I is the general-purpose cement most often used for residential construction.

Portland cement comes in gray, white, and buff varieties, and is usually sold in 94-pound bags (1 cubic foot). Materials called admixtures are combined with cement to modify its properties. For example, air-entraining agents improve concrete's resistance to freezing and the effects of salt deposits. (Type I, II, and III cements are available with air-entrainers mixed in and are designated with the letter A after the type number.) Other admixtures include accelerators, which speed up the hardening process; retarders, which slow it down; plasticizers, which improve concrete flow; and pigments, which add color to white cement.

If cement is allowed to get wet during storage, it will begin to harden. Always store cement bags off the ground—on wooden skids, for example—and cover them with plastic.

The second ingredient in concrete is a combination of coarse and fine aggregates. Coarse aggregate is gravel or crushed stone sold by the cubic foot or yard. The mix should include particles ranging from ¼ inch to 1½ inches in diameter. The particles should not be larger than one-fourth of the concrete's thickness. Fine aggregate consists of sand particles measuring less than ¼ inch in diameter. Concrete sand, called bank-run sand, should be free of silt and contaminants. Never use beach sand in the mix because it contains impurities.

The final ingredient in concrete is water, which triggers the chemical reaction that gradually hardens concrete. Water for mixing concrete should be clean and free of organic matter, oil, acid, and other impurities.

Estimating Concrete

The amount of concrete you need dictates whether you should buy prepackaged materials, mix your own by hand or machine, or have ready-mix concrete delivered to you. To calculate the volume of a rectangular footing, wall, or slab, multiply length by width by thickness (all in feet or fractions of a foot) and divide by 27 to obtain the total volume in cubic yards, which is

CHAPTER 3 Concrete

ESTIMATING SITE-MIXED AND READY-MIX CONCRETE ORDERS

To estimate how much concrete to mix or order, use this chart or total up the volume inside the forms in cubic feet (length x height x width) and divide the result by 27 to convert into the standard of cubic yards. Some contractors build in a reasonable excess factor of about 8% by changing the conversion factor to 25. On ready-mix orders it's wise to round up your estimate, because falling short can ruin a job.

CONCRETE COVERAGE CHART

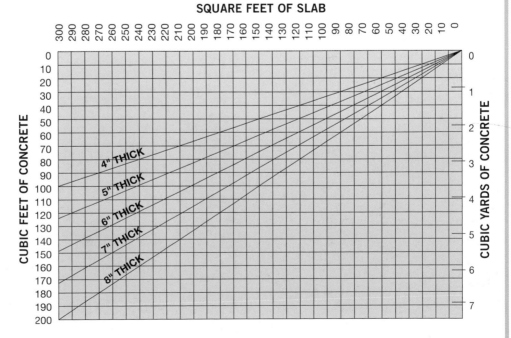

how ready-mix is usually sold. To figure the volume of a cylinder in cubic yards, multiply the square of its radius in feet by *pi* (3.14), multiply the result by the cylinder's height, and divide by 27. To calculate overall volume, break down irregular shapes into rectangles, triangles, and portions of circles. To allow for waste and irregularities in concrete thickness, add about 5 percent to your order.

Mix Proportions

Concrete-mix proportions vary depending on the intended use of the concrete and the weather conditions. Especially important is the water-to-cement ratio. Too much water will weaken the concrete, and too little will make it unworkable.

Site-mixed concrete is typically 1 part cement, 2½ parts sand, 3 parts coarse aggregate, and about 5 gallons of water per bag of cement. But there are exceptions to the rule. For example, add more water on hot, dry days to prevent the wet mix from drying out prematurely and weakening the concrete.

With ready-mix concrete, you don't have to worry about proportions. But when you place an order, you do need to specify the volume needed and its intended use. The supplier can then determine the required compressive strength (load-bearing capacity after 28 days), minimum cement content, maximum aggregate size, and any required admixtures.

If you're mixing concrete yourself, measure out the dry ingredients carefully in a clean container and mix them thoroughly with a mason's hoe. Slowly add water, and pull the dry ingredients from the sides into the water. Keep adding water and mixing until ridges cut in the concrete with the hoe hold their shape. Hand-mixing concrete is hard work. You can spare yourself some of the effort by renting a small power mixer.

Mixing Concrete On Site

If you need less than 1 cubic yard of concrete or if ready-mix is not available, you can mix your own concrete on site either by hand or with a power mixer. When mixing concrete by any method, prevent skin irritation by wearing long sleeves, long pants, and waterproof gloves.

Prepackaged Concrete Mixes. For very small projects you may want to purchase a packaged concrete mix. These combine cement, sand, and gravel in the correct proportions and require only the addition of water to create fresh concrete. The most commonly available sizes are 40-, 60-, and 80-pound bags. A 40-pound bag makes about ⅓ cubic foot of concrete, a 60-pound bag makes about ½ cubic foot, and an 80-pound bag, about ⅔ cubic foot.

While convenient, prepackaged mixes are too expensive to use for everything, you may be able to use them for the small projects. If you use pre-mixed bags, you can pick them up yourself from

Preparing and Testing Site-Mixed Concrete

Once you add portland cement, sand, and aggregate as required for your job, thoroughly mix the dry ingredients.

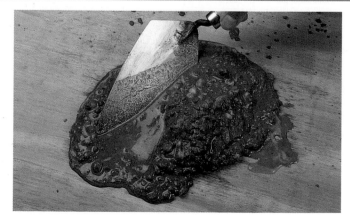

If a sample batch of concrete is too wet, ridges made in the mix with a trowel won't hold their shape.

the supplier or spend a little extra money to have them delivered. If you pick them up, make sure that none of the bags have already hardened. However the concrete arrives at your house, be sure to store it in an elevated and dry location. The bags can be stored outdoors if they are covered with plastic sheeting or a waterproof tarp. If you live in a humid climate, buy the concrete no more than one or two days before you intend to use it.

Mixing Concrete by Hand

If you want to use air-entrained concrete or an air-entraining admixture, you cannot hand-mix because you won't be able to stir vigorously enough to produce the proper air entrainment.

To hand-mix concrete, start with a square-point shovel or mason's hoe, thoroughly combining the dry ingredients. You can mix the ingredients in a clean wheelbarrow, a plastic mixing tub, or a similar type of container.

Water content is crucial, so note that the sand used to make the concrete should be wet but not completely saturated. The sand should hold a ball shape in your hand. If it's too wet, the ball will drip water and won't hold its shape. If the sand is too dry, it will absorb too much water, weakening the concrete. Wet it thoroughly with a garden hose the day before beginning work. Cover your sand pile with a sheet of plastic when you're not working. This will prevent the sand from drying out and altering the overall mix ratios.

USING READY-MIX CONCRETE

There are several advantages to ordering ready-mix concrete, aside from the fact that you don't have to mix yards of the stuff by hand. Ready-mix trucks can deliver concrete tailored to your job and the weather, so you can pour even during a heat wave. Also, ready-mix concrete is available with an additive that produces microscopic air bubbles in the mix—air-entrainment, resulting in concrete that is more resistant to cracking than that you can mix on site. Finally, extension chutes can be swiveled to pour concrete where it's needed.

In the ideal situation, extension chutes can direct concrete into the braced forms.

If the sample batch is too dry, you won't be able to make ridges, and the mix will not be cohesive.

When mixed correctly, the ridges will hold most of their shape, and only a little water will be visible.

Forming and Reinforcing

Wet concrete is poured into forms, which hold and shape the concrete until it hardens. Usually made of lumber and (in the case of wall forms) plywood sheathing, forms must be level, plumb, and strong enough to withstand the weight of the concrete pushing against them. Forms for edges of slabs and continuous wall footings are typically made of two-by lumber.

Form boards should be free of holes and other flaws that might weaken them or mar the concrete's surface. The boards are set on edge and braced every 3 to 4 feet with wooden stakes driven firmly into the ground. To make the forms easier to remove, fasten the boards to the stakes using screws or double-headed nails. Wherever two boards butt together, screw a plywood gusset across the outside of each joint.

Forms for footings and slabs are usually built on site. More complicated forms for perimeter wall foundations are either site-built or constructed using prefabricated panels rented from concrete form suppliers.

Continuous-Footing Forms. Foundation walls rest on concrete footings set below the frost line to avoid frost-heave damage. The footing height should be the same as the thickness of the wall, or a minimum of 8 inches. The footing width should be twice that of the wall, or a minimum of 16 inches.

Concrete for wall footings is generally poured into wooden forms anchored by 1x4 stakes driven into the ground and braced with 1x4 spreaders nailed across board tops every 4 to 6 feet. A chamfered 2x4 suspended from the spreaders down the center of the form creates a depression, or keyway, in the footing that will help secure a poured concrete wall.

Wall Foundation Forms. Install basement wall formwork after the footings have cured. The forms are usually made of smooth, knot-free plywood sheathing supported by 2x4 studs, braces, and horizontal members called wales. Wire ties hold the plywood walls together. Wood spreaders keep them a fixed distance apart.

COMPACTING SOIL

Concrete is so heavy that in time it compresses loose soil underneath it. Uneven soil settling creates stress in the concrete that can lead to cracking. The best way to avoid the problem is to leave the subgrade undisturbed when you excavate a footing trench. Remove sod and topsoil, but leave a solid, untouched bed of soil on which the footing will rest. Because this isn't always possible, any soil that has been removed and replaced must be tamped solid with either a hand tamper or a vibration compactor.

Building Formed Footings

TOOLS
- Measuring tape and string
- Shovel
- Hammer
- Level and clamps
- Power drill-driver

MATERIALS
- Two-by form boards and stakes
- One-by spreaders
- Plywood gussets

3 **Check the form boards for level**, *clamp them temporarily, and nail or screw them in place.*

A 4x4 post makes an effective, if rudimentary, hand tamper. Rent a vibrating compactor for large projects.

1 *Excavate the sod and soil* within your string lines to a depth below the local frost line.

2 *Drive pointed 2x4 stakes* every 4 ft. or so and on each side of corners to support the form boards.

4 *Secure butt joints* in form boards with plywood gussets screwed across the exterior faces.

5 *Fasten 1x2 spreaders* across the forms to help resist the force of the concrete.

Joints in Concrete

Construction Joints. These joints are installed wherever a concrete pour is interrupted for more than 30 minutes or stopped at the end of the day. Within the formwork, the section being poured is closed off with a temporary stop board. It is then screeded and floated.

For slabs that are only 4 inches thick, a straight-edged butt joint is adequate, but for thicker slabs, a keyed tongue-and-groove joint may be used to help transfer loads between adjoining sections of concrete. The tongue-and-groove construction allows the slab surface to remain level, but the sections can expand and contract independently.

A tongue-and-groove joint is shaped by attaching a beveled wood, metal, or molded-plastic form along the middle of the temporary stop board. The edge of the pour takes this beveled shape. The subsequent pour takes an inverse shape. The oil coating prevents a bond between the pours. After the second pour has set, tool a control joint above the construction joint.

Isolation Joints. These joints are an important element in the formwork. They consist of strips that separate new concrete from existing adjacent construction and other slabs that might expand and contract differently, or experience different soil settlement or other movement.

If fresh concrete is not separated from these elements by an isolation joint, a crack could form where the two meet. Isolation joints are ¼- to ½-inch-wide molded fiber, cork, or rubber strip dividers set ¼ inch below the concrete's surface.

Edging Joints. When the water sheen is gone from the first floating, it's time to run an edger along the forms. Edging gives the pour rounded edges that resist cracking. But first use the point of a small trowel to cut the top inch or so of concrete away from the face of the form, so that the form will pull away from the concrete easily when it is removed, without breaking the edge. Then run an edging trowel around the entire slab perimeter to form an attractive finished

Stamping tools can create a variety of shallow grid patterns so that concrete resembles pavers.

Forming Curves

TOOLS

- Spade
- Hammer
- 4-foot level
- Power drill-driver
- Garden hose or stakes and string

MATERIALS

- Scrap 2x4 lumber
- ⅛-inch hardboard
- Screws and nails

1 *Lay out the curve* using a garden hose or stakes and string. Excavate the sod to your layout line.

2 *Make form stakes* from pieces of one-by or two-by lumber with the ends trimmed to a point.

3 *Use a level* long enough to span the pour, and set consistent stake heights through the corner.

4 *Screw ⅛-in.-thick hardboard* to the insides of the stakes to create a consistent curve.

5 *Reinforce the curve* against the force of poured concrete with extra stakes outside the form.

edge. Run the edger back and forth to smooth the surface, without gouging the concrete. Raise the front edge slightly when moving the edger forward, and raise the back edge when moving the tool backward.

Control Joints. Shrinkage cracks in concrete are controlled by control joints tooled into the surface. Control joints allow the concrete to crack in straight lines at planned locations. They can be hand-tooled into fresh concrete with a special jointing tool; cut into partially cured concrete with a circular saw fitted with a masonry blade; or formed with fixed divider strips of wood or of specially molded fiber.

(When the divider strips are used at full slab depth, the control joint is also an isolation joint.) Tooled and saw-cut control joints must be at least one-fourth of the thickness of the concrete. This weakens the section, causing cracks to occur at the bottom of the joints where they will be inconspicuous.

It is best to subdivide concrete into panels that are square, rather than elongated. Rectangular areas more than one and one half times as long as they are wide are prone to cracking in the middle across the width. On a sidewalk, concrete will be less likely to crack if the joints form square panels spaced 3 feet apart.

Building Formed Piers vs. Formless Piers

Dig below the frost line to prevent heaving, and insert a form tube cut to extend about 4 in. above grade.

Plumb and level the form, and gradually add dirt to backfill the pier, compacting it around the tube.

Use a posthole digger to excavate a hole for a formless pier where the walls of the hole serve as the formwork.

Measure to make sure that the base of the pier will rest below the minimum frost depth for your region.

Formed and Formless Piers

Concrete piers are used mainly to support decks, porches, and outbuildings. Piers are susceptible to shifting out of plumb in areas with freeze-thaw cycles or shifting soil. So whether you use formless piers or tube forms, you need to dig below the local frost depth to prevent heaving. In most cases, you'll also need to install a galvanized bracket to keep a post or girder securely in place.

Holes for piers need to be deep and narrow. They are best dug with a power auger or a hand posthole digger—a shovel will dig a hole with too wide of a mouth. Minimize settling by digging down to the required depth and pounding the dirt at the bottom of the hole with the end of a 2x4. The concrete pier must rest on a solid base.

If the sides of the holes aren't crumbling, you could use them as rough forms. In that case, build a box staked at ground level to contain the concrete above grade. However, to avoid mixing in dirt, you can use lightweight form tubes, cut to the height you need and backfilled.

To determine the cubic footage of a cylinder form, multiply (in inches) the radius (half the diameter) by itself, and that number by its height, and that number by 3.14. Divide the result by 1,728 to estimate in cubic feet.

Pour concrete *into the form, level the surface, and insert a J-bolt, leaving the threads exposed.*

After the concrete sets, *you can attach hardware that connects the concrete pier to a post or girder.*

Fill the hole *with the concrete mix, taking care not to dislodge dirt from the walls of the excavation.*

Install galvanized post hardware, *typically with a pin into the pier, and adjust it before the concrete hardens.*

CHAPTER 3 Concrete

Reinforcing

Steel reinforcement strengthens concrete and reduces cracking. Reinforcing bar (rebar) used in residential construction ranges in diameter from ¼ to 1 inch and has ridges on its surface to provide a better bond with concrete. Rebar is numbered according to its diameter in eighths of an inch. A #3 bar, for example, has a ⅜-inch diameter. Reinforcing bars are stronger than reinforcing mesh and are used for concrete that will carry a heavy load, such as footings and foundation walls.

Reinforcing mesh (also called welded wire) is made from a grid of steel wires, usually 6, 8, or 10 gauge. The mesh comes in rolls and is used primarily in flat work such as sidewalks, patios, and driveways. The rolls are generally 5 by 150 feet. The mesh can be cut with large fencing pliers or electrical wire cutters.

You must flatten the mesh thoroughly to prevent it from moving to the top or bottom of the pour. Flat sheets of mesh may be easier to work with than the rolls. Where the form is wider than the mesh, overlap sections by at least 6 inches and bind them together with wire. It's important to set the mesh approximately mid-height in the pour, keeping it back about 2 inches from the perimeter forms.

REINFORCING CONCRETE FOOTINGS

Steel reinforcement bar (rebar, for short) is used to strengthen concrete, and is typically required by code in footings and foundations that carry heavy loads. The bars come in 20-foot lengths and in diameters ranging from ¼ to 1 inch. A typical 16-inch-wide footing for a house often requires two continuous ½-inch bars set about 8 inches apart down the center of the form. (Check local codes for details.) It's important to elevate the rebar (about 2 inches) so that it rests in the concrete instead of on the ground. You can support it with bricks or small fittings called chairs.

Support rebar *about 2 in. off the ground with pieces of brick, block, or small fittings (chairs).*

REINFORCING CONCRETE SLABS

Reinforcing mesh, generally known as welded wire, is made of steel wires woven or welded into a grid that is used to strengthen concrete slabs and reduce cracking. Like rebar, welded wire should be elevated so that it rests in the slab instead of on the ground. You can rest the reinforcement on special fittings, called chairs, or pieces of brick, block, or stone. If you need to reinforce an irregularly shaped slab, overlap sections of mesh at least 6 inches and bind them together with wire ties. Also keep welded wire back an inch or two from the outside edges of a slab.

Welded wire mesh *comes in rolls or sheets. You need to thoroughly flatten the mesh inside forms.*

Poured concrete with color additives can make sturdy and decorative outdoor walls.

Secure rebar *to masonry or special supports with wire ties to keep them from moving during the pour.*

Lap and wire-tie adjoining rebar *at least 12 in. around corners to provide unbroken support.*

Cut back mesh reinforcement *so that it is separated from form boards by about 2 in. on all sides.*

Use brick or block sections *to support welded wire roughly 2 in. above the base of the excavation.*

Pouring

Regardless of whether you mix your own or have ready-mix delivered to your site, you must work quickly when pouring concrete in formwork. If your project is large enough to require a delivery of ready-mix concrete, you will probably need to enlist some friends to help with the pour.

Be sure to wear rubber boots, gloves, and protective clothing, because prolonged contact with fresh concrete mixtures may irritate your skin.

Before pouring concrete, check the formwork. You may want to add extra braces in key locations to resist the increased force of concrete pouring from a ready-mix truck chute.

Once you're sure that the forms are ready, spray the inside surfaces and the soil or gravel base with water. This will prevent water from being drawn out of the concrete, which can produce a weak and crumbly surface. Moistening is especially important on a day that's warm and windy. Also be sure to spray any metal reinforcements, which can become blisteringly hot under a summer sun and burn off a great deal of moisture from the mix.

Moving the Mix

For large projects such as driveways, have at least two wheelbarrows for transporting the concrete to the forms. Lay 2x12s across lawn areas to protect them from the weight of the wheelbarrow, and build ramps over the forms so that you don't bump them out of place.

Begin placing concrete piles in the farthest corner of the forms, making them slightly higher than the formwork. Move the concrete with hoes and shovels. You may need to raise the wire mesh with a hammer claw to ensure that it stays approximately in the middle of the pour. During the pour, repeatedly consolidate the concrete by moving a shovel, hoe, or 2x4 up and down to release air bubbles. This is especially important near the edges and in corners. However, don't overdo it. If you overwork the concrete, the water will separate and rise to the top, weakening the mix. Further settle the concrete against the perimeter by tapping the outside of the form boards with a hammer.

Once the form is filled and tamped, begin screeding, or striking off, the surface level with the top of the forms. Use a length of 2x4 slightly wider than the forms. Try to use a straight piece of lumber, but if there is a bow to the wood, screed with the convex side up. Move the screed back and forth as you slide it along the tops of the forms. Keep both ends pressed down on top of the forms to force all of the aggregate into the concrete. Fill hollow areas with a shovelful of concrete, and level them. For a large pour, two people can begin screeding as concrete is placed ahead of them.

FORMING PIPE SLEEVES

Before pouring concrete into foundation forms, install blockouts, or barriers, to accommodate electrical conduits and gas and water pipes. Create a blockout by drilling holes through the forms and sliding through a piece of PVC pipe. Leave the pipes long, and trim them flush once the forms are stripped. Pipe diameters should be slightly over-size to allow easy access.

Use a hole saw or saber saw to cut holes matching the pipe diameter.

Insert plastic pipe through the holes to provide access for utilities.

Pouring Footing Forms

TOOLS
- Shovel
- Trowel
- Screed board
- Pliers

MATERIALS
- Bricks or rebar chairs
- Wire ties
- Concrete
- Anchor bolts

1 *Transport concrete* in a wheelbarrow, and shovel it into place without disrupting the overlapped rebar.

2 *Fill the forms completely,* tamping the concrete as you go to eliminate voids and air bubbles.

3 *To form a smooth, sound edge,* use a trowel to fill corners, sliding it along the sides of the forms.

4 *Move a 2x4 screed* back and forth across the forms to smooth and strike off excess concrete.

5 *Embed anchor bolts* in the concrete at 4 ft. centers and within 12 in. of each corner or opening.

Finishing and Curing

Floating is the first step in the finishing of concrete and is done immediately after screeding. Initial floating with a bull float or a darby depresses large aggregates and knocks down small ridges. To use a bull float, push it across the surface with the front edge raised a bit. When pulling it back, keep it's blade flat to cut off bumps and fill any holes. At the end of each stroke, lift the float and move it over, creating a parallel stroke.

A darby is smaller and easier to control. Use two hands to move it in sweeping arcs across the concrete surface. Do not allow the edges or end of the tool to dig into the concrete.

After the first floating, wait for the water sheen to leave the concrete surface. If you begin edging and further finishing while there is water on the surface, the concrete quality, especially at the surface, may be reduced. Of course, if you wait too long, the concrete will be unworkable.

Curing Concrete

Concrete must be kept moist, generally for seven days, to allow the portland cement in the mix to cure and harden properly. When moisture is pulled from the concrete too quickly, the surface can develop hairline cracks or have a chalky residue. Hot, dry, or windy weather increases evaporation, making it more difficult to keep the slab moist. Cold weather requires special precautions for curing.

There are many different ways to cure concrete properly. You can cover and seal the surface completely with large sheets of plastic or lay burlap over the surface and spray it with a garden hose twice daily to keep it wet. Another option is to set a sprinkler to continually but gradually pool water on the surface. But first be sure that the surface has hardened enough to resist being marred by the spray.

Concrete hardens best between 50 and 70 degrees F. If concrete freezes before at least two days of curing it will be very weak and basically ruined. If you expect cold weather, apply a heavy layer of straw or blankets covered with plastic sheeting. In very hot weather, simply keep the concrete moist.

Removing the Forms

After the concrete has cured for at least one day the forms can be removed. But prying or hammering can damage the pour. This is why it's best to secure forms with double-headed nails, which are easy to pull, or better yet, with screws that are easy to back out. After the forms are stripped, the concrete will continue to cure and reach nearly its full strength in about a month. But it is safe to walk on and use the surface after one week.

Finishing Concrete Edges and Joints

Form a slab perimeter with an edging trowel. Run it slowly back and forth to smooth and round the edge.

Form control joints with a jointing trowel run against a squared-up 2x4 serving as a straightedge guide.

CURING CONCRETE

There are several ways to keep concrete moist, which is key to the curing process during which concrete hardens. You can moisten the concrete with a garden hose and then cover it with large plastic sheets to retard evaporation. (Weigh down the edges of the sheets with bricks.) Another way to lock in moisture is to apply a curing compound to the damp surface with a paint roller. You can also cover the concrete with water-saturated burlap or canvas. But you will need to keep the coverings wet during the curing period by adding water periodically (particularly in hot, dry weather) with a lawn sprinkler or soaking hose.

Spray the surface of finished concrete lightly but thoroughly with water from a garden hose.

A curing compound applied to concrete with a paint roller will retard moisture loss during curing.

Covering fresh concrete with overlapped plastic sheeting can also lock in moisture.

The jointing trowel leaves a smooth groove in the surface, but you may need to clear out the interior seam.

Use a float to smooth the surface and clear any marks or extra material left by edging or jointing.

CHAPTER 3 Concrete

Maintenance and Repair

Concrete structures and surfaces are not easily demolished and replaced, which makes proper maintenance and repair a wise alternative.

Many problems arise from exposure to repeated cycles of freezing and thawing, which can cause cracks and spalling, among other problems. Uneven settlement of the soil beneath the concrete is another common cause of cracking. General repairs (shown here and on the next two pages) involve cleaning out cracks and undercutting them if possible so that the patching compound embeds in the old surface.

When a larger section of concrete has been damaged, such as an entire panel of a sidewalk or patio, you will probably have to demolish and replace the section. Break up the existing concrete with a sledgehammer, remove the pieces, level the ground, install formwork, and then pour and finish the concrete.

Preventive Maintenance

Concrete is absorbant and can be damaged by repeated freezing and thawing. Clear water-repellent coatings, available in many proprietary mixes, can help decrease water absorption and

Repairing Large Cracks

TOOLS

- 2-pound hammer and cold chisel
- Goggles
- Whisk broom or shop vac
- Wire brush
- Trowels

MATERIALS

- Concrete patch mix
- Plastic sheeting (for curing)

1 *To make a secure patch,* use a cold chisel to undercut the surface on each side of the crack.

2 *Wire-brush the crack* (and sweep out debris) to scour the edges and create a good bond surface.

3 *Use a pointed trowel* to force cement into the undercut areas before filling and finishing.

FIXING SMALL CRACKS

To repair small cracks, start by cleaning out dirt and debris with a whisk broom. Concrete repair caulk provides a quick fix for minor cracks and prevents further damage. But it is only a temporary repair. To patch cracks that keep opening, under-cut the edges with a cold chisel, and fill with flexible, exterior-grade caulk or hydraulic cement that swells as it hardens.

Brush cracks clean, and fill them with flexible concrete caulk.

Patching Broken Steps

TOOLS

- 2-pound hammer and cold chisel
- Goggles
- Work gloves
- Hammer and square
- Trowel

MATERIALS

- Form boards
- 1x2 braces and nails
- Mortar mix

1 **Wire-brush the damaged area** to remove debris. Then build a plywood form to square off the step.

2 **Drive a few concrete nails,** and coat the area with a bonding agent to help patch material adhere.

3 **Nails driven halfway** into the old step are covered by patch mix and smoothed out level with the form.

reduce repairs. Concrete slabs are often treated to reduce staining from dirt and other substances.

Water repellents are available in both water- and solvent-based formulations. The water-based mixes need to be applied more often but emit less toxic fumes and are safer for both you and the environment. Both types of coatings are thin and nonelastic, so they will not waterproof cracks in a concrete surface.

Always test a coating on a small, inconspicuous area before beginning work. Also plan to reapply the clear coating every three to seven years, depending on the specific product and the manufacturer's recommendations.

Spot-Cleaning Concrete

Use a commercial absorbent *or sawdust to lift deep oil stains. Work the absorbent around with a brick.*

DIAGNOSING CONCRETE PROBLEMS

Crazing, or shallow surface cracks, and spalling, or surface pitting, are caused by over-floating the finished surface. This brings too many fine particles to the surface, creating a weak layer of concrete. To prevent such problems, mix dry ingredients thoroughly before adding water, and don't overwork the finish. Another problem, oxidizing iron, causes rust-colored stains. Clean them with a solution of oxalic acid crystals, water, and ammonium bifluoride. Always wear face and hand protection when mixing an acid solution, and follow manufacturer's safety precautions.

CRAZING

Replacing Expansion Joints

When fiberboard and lumber *used to form expansion joints in concrete wears away, clean out the debris.*

Before resealing the joint, *sweep out old pieces of lumber or clean out the seam with a wet-dry vac.*

Use a brush and concrete cleaner to scrub out stains. Then wash the entire surface before sealing.

Applying a clear concrete sealer improves the appearance of a concrete driveway and helps it shed water.

SPALLING

OXIDATION

To allow for some shifting and to minimize cracking, pack a strip of foam backer rod into the joint.

Cover the backer rod and seal the joint against the weather with a layer of self-leveling urethane sealant.

CHAPTER 3 Concrete

Many types of heavy walls require a concrete footing, including the walls of a house. This project includes the basics of forming and pouring to cover most situations, such as building a footing for a mortared stone wall. Footing design generally follows a basic proportion: its depth should equal the thickness of the wall above, and its width should be twice the wall's width. In a typical house footing, the pour is 8 inches deep and 16 inches wide, and it supports an 8-inch-thick foundation wall of block or poured concrete. To strengthen the footing, lay two rebars in the lower third of the pour, set in about 2 inches from the sides. House footings are governed by codes that include the exact size and placement of rebar and the depth of the pour. To avoid heaving, house footings must be poured below the average frost depth in your area.

Concrete Footing

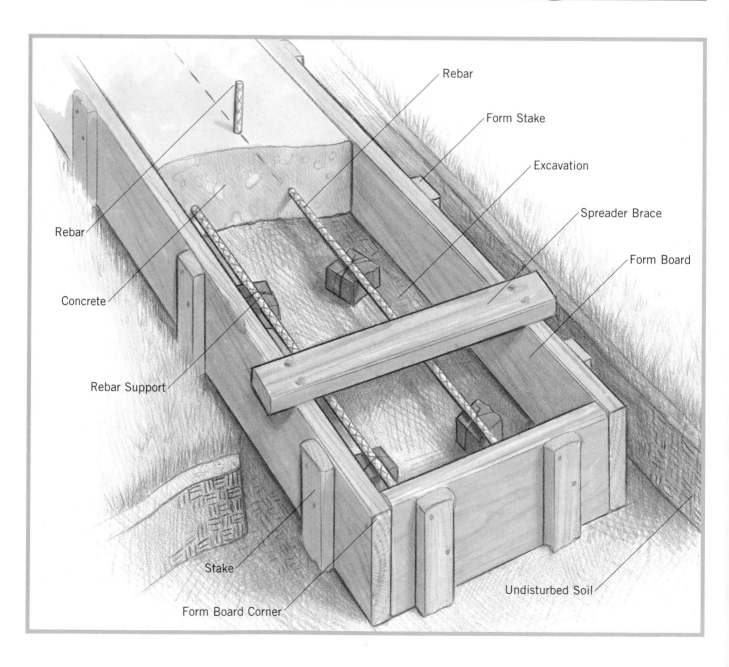

Concrete Footing Installation

TOOLS

- Work gloves
- Spade and shovel
- Hammer
- Mason's trowel
- Pliers
- Spirit level
- Wheelbarrow
- Measuring tape

MATERIALS

- Batter boards
- Form boards and stakes
- Concrete mix
- Spray paint
- String
- Bricks or wire chairs
- Rebar
- Nails

SMART JOB TIP

A few feet beyond the area where you'll be working, build sturdy batter boards that won't shift. Once you make a careful layout for the footing and drive nails to mark the lines, remove the strings so that they won't be in your way. You can restring them later to align the forms.

CHAPTER 3 Concrete

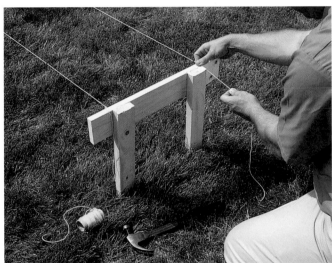

1 *Set up batter boards* and run strings between them to lay out the excavation for your footing.

2 *Transfer the string lines* to the ground with spray paint to guide your sod removal and digging.

3 *After undercutting the sod* along the paint lines with a spade, roll it up and save it for use elsewhere.

4 *If your project* will be attached to a permanent structure, excavate below the frost line.

DOUBLE-HEADED NAILS

Many homeowners and builders use screws and a drill-driver to fasten temporary parts, such as spreaders on footing forms. But if you use an old fashioned hammer, save yourself some time and trouble by driving double-headed nails. You can drive them home, and the second head still protrudes, making it easy to pull the nails as you strip the forms.

Hammer the double-headed nail just as you would any other nail.

The second head makes removing these nails fast and easy.

5 *Measure down from ground level to the bottom of the excavation to be sure it's deep enough.*

6 *Build and install the form over compacted soil, and check to be sure the form is level.*

9 *Tack spreaders across the form to prevent the sides from being pushed apart by the concrete.*

10 *Mix concrete in a wheelbarrow or a rented power mixer, or have ready-mix concrete delivered.*

SUPPORTING REBAR

Rebar should be supported in the bottom third of the pour. It should not protrude from the bottom of the concrete. To set rebar in the proper position (and keep it in place as you pour concrete) use either half bricks or specially made wire chairs. Chairs are better because they hold the rebar in position and will not soak up moisture from the pour as bricks will.

Tie rebar to half bricks with wire to keep it from slipping as your pour.

Wire holders, called chairs, have indents to hold the rebar.

7 Drive stakes around the form to hold it in position. Recheck for level, and screw them to the form.

8 Support rebar on half bricks or wire chairs, secured with wire to prevent shifting as you pour.

11 Move a screed board back and forth across the form to fill any low spots and smooth the mix.

12 Install rebar in the footing to code. You can later tie this to rebar in the wall you build on top.

A concrete pier is a fundamental component of construction that takes the place of a continuous foundation. Piers are commonly used under decks, porches, sheds, and other outbuildings for which you don't need a solid masonry wall between the ground and the floor of the structure. For a deck or porch, for example, it's practical to install piers at intervals that you can span with girders to support the floor framing. To build piers, you can simply dump concrete into a hole. But that approach often weakens the pier as dirt gets mixed with the concrete. You can instead build your own forms of plywood to hold the concrete. But the most efficient system employs prefabricated tube forms, which are lightweight and easy to cut to length. Like full foundations, piers must reach below the frost line to avoid the force of heaving.

Concrete Pier

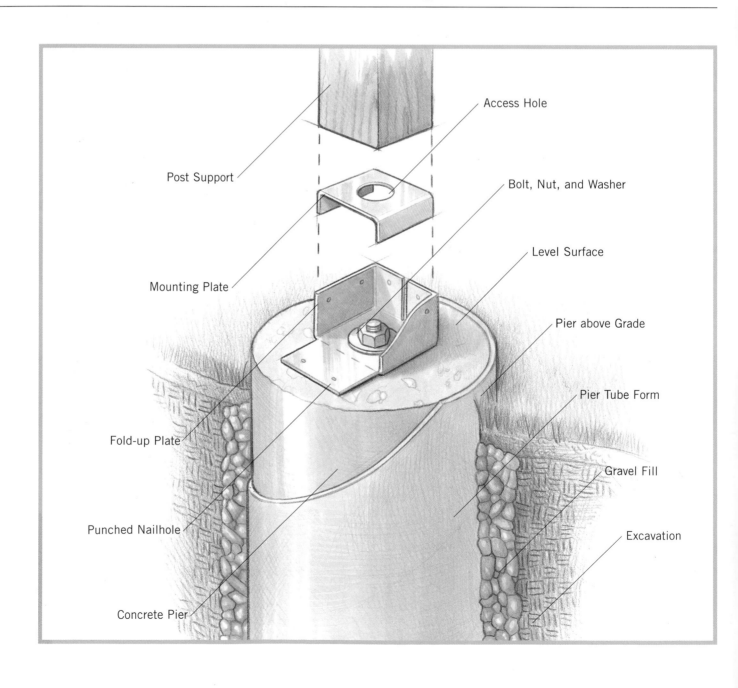

Post Support

Mounting Plate

Fold-up Plate

Punched Nailhole

Concrete Pier

Access Hole

Bolt, Nut, and Washer

Level Surface

Pier above Grade

Pier Tube Form

Gravel Fill

Excavation

Concrete Pier Installation

TOOLS

- Work gloves
- Posthole digger
- Measuring tape
- Saws
- Level
- Wheelbarrow and shovel
- Wrench
- Trowel
- Hammer
- Clamp

MATERIALS

- Prefab tube form
- Gravel
- Concrete mix
- Anchor bolt or threaded rod
- Wire
- Post-holder hardware
- 1x4 braces and 1x2 stakes
- Nails

SMART JOB TIP

Prefabricated forms are available in several diameters. An 8- or 10-inch tube is generally large enough to form piers that support posts in deck projects. But you'll need to check with the local building department about pier size requirements for larger loads.

1 *Use a posthole digger* to excavate a hole just slightly wider than the diameter of the form.

2 *Measure the depth of the hole* to be sure that the concrete will reach below the frost line.

3 *Cut the reinforced cardboard tube* with a saw, so it will stand a few inches above grade.

4 *Level the top of the tube form,* and check the tube walls for plumb before backfilling.

BUILDING YOUR OWN FORMS

For large piers you can pour concrete into the excavation, and form only the projection a few inches above grade. This approach can save time but could create a weak pier if a lot of dirt mixes with the concrete as you pour it into the hole. The other drawback is that you probably will wind up pouring more concrete than necessary to fill the irregular excavation.

Frame the hole with 2x4s or 2x6s staked in a level position.

Consolidate the mix, add a center anchor, and smooth the surface.

5 *Stabilize the form* by backfilling with gravel or dirt. The tube should extend a few inches above grade.

6 *Mix your concrete* in a wheelbarrow or mixing tub, and fill to the top of the tube.

9 *Use wires twisted around nails* to hold the rod or anchor bolt in place as the concrete hardens.

10 *When the pier has cured,* you can attach post- or girder-holding hardware to the rod or bolt.

POURING PIERS AROUND POSTS

nother approach is to set your posts in the excavations and pour concrete around them. This saves the trouble of forming altogether and is the approach often used for fence posts. The drawback is that part of the post is in the ground, where even some pressure-treated woods can eventually rot. For decks, porches, and outbuildings, it's better to set posts on top of piers.

Place gravel in the hole *as a footing for the pressure-treated post.*

Brace the post *in plumb position, and pour the concrete around it.*

7 **Smooth the top** *with a trowel after consolidating the mix by inserting a board or a shovel handle.*

8 **Insert an anchor bolt or threaded rod** *so it protrudes from the center of the concrete form.*

11 **Set the post in the hardware support,** *check for plumb, and add staked braces in two directions.*

12 **Nail through the galvanized flanges** *on the hardware to lock the post in place on the pier.*

A concrete slab is one of the most basic types of masonry construction and is employed in various locations. Using the same basic procedures you'll find in this project, you can build a slab to stand alone as a walkway or patio. Slabs are also used on basement floors and to support small sheds and other outbuildings. Although many houses are built on slabs, they require a perimeter footing. Building a slab is not difficult, but mixing the concrete can be, particularly on a large project. For large projects you should order by the cubic yard from a ready-mix company that will deliver the mix ready to pour. If you plan to mix your own concrete for a small project, remember that one wheelbarrow-sized batch generally makes less than 3 cubic feet. You would need approximately nine wheelbarrow batches to make just 1 cubic yard.

Concrete Slab

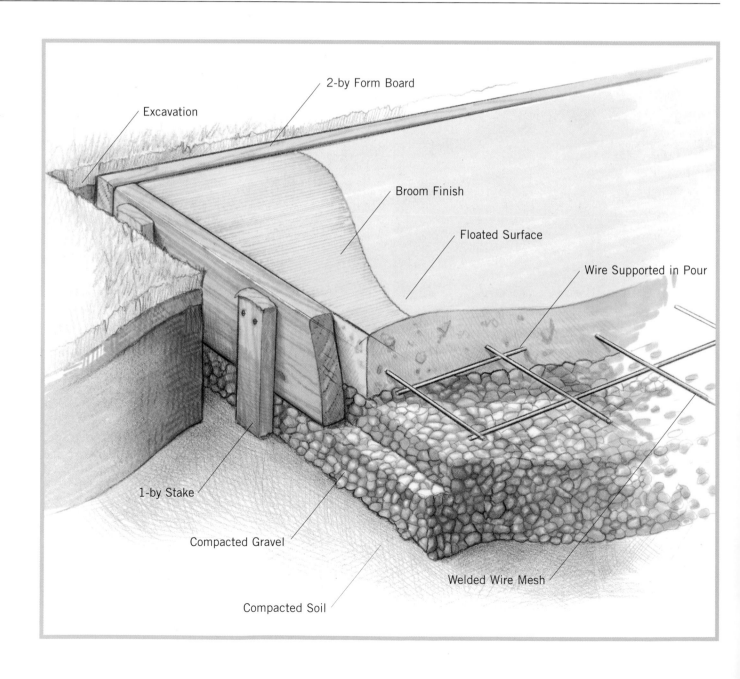

Excavation

2-by Form Board

Broom Finish

Floated Surface

Wire Supported in Pour

1-by Stake

Compacted Gravel

Welded Wire Mesh

Compacted Soil

Concrete Slab Installation

TOOLS

- Work gloves
- Vibrating power tamper
- Line level and pencil
- Pry bar
- Broom and rake
- Spirit level
- Wheelbarrow
- Power drill-driver
- Bull float and hose
- Edging and jointing trowels

MATERIALS

- Mason's string
- Welded-wire mesh
- Gravel
- Concrete mix
- Burlap
- Lumber for forms, screeding boards, and stakes

SMART JOB TIP

Although a reinforced-concrete slab seems nearly indestructible, it can crack unless you build it over solid, compacted soil. For best results, rent a vibrating power tamper that consolidates soil. Use it on the dirt subbase and then on the gravel base before pouring the concrete.

CHAPTER 3 Concrete

1 *Mark outside the perimeter* of the slab with spray paint. Then cut and roll up the sod to reuse.

2 *Excavate below the frost line,* and drive stakes to mark the outside line of the form boards.

3 *Use a line level* strung between corner stakes to establish the level (and drain slope) of the slab.

4 *Use a large steel pry bar* to remove any large rocks that would interfere with the concrete.

FORMING SLABS ON A SLOPE

You can regrade the work area to create a level excavation for a slab. But in many cases it's more practical to accommodate a gentle slope by increasing the depth in a small area of the pour. Where the ground falls away, drive longer form stakes and maintain level with the main form board. Then add an angled filler board below to contain the gravel and concrete.

Run the top form boards to a pair of long stakes at the low corner.

Fill in the slope with angled boards attached with extra stakes.

5 *Fill any large depressions* in the excavation with gravel to save on concrete.

6 *Use a mechanical tamper* to compact gravel recesses and the dirt floor of the excavation.

9 *If you need to butt form boards* on a long run, join them with screws over an extra-wide stake.

10 *Screed the gravel bed* so that it is roughly even with the bottom edges of the form boards.

USING WELDED WIRE

Even on a small slab or narrow walkway, you should reinforce the pour with welded wire. On larger projects you can overlap sheets by at least one grid and join the sections with wire ties (near right). Ideally, the mesh should rest in the lower third of the slab. On large jobs you can rest the wire on supports. On small jobs, simply lift the mesh (far right) as you pour.

Overlap welded wire on large slabs, and tie the sheets together.

On small jobs, lift the wire off the gravel as you pour the concrete.

7 **Rake out a 4- to 6-in. bed of gravel.** Reset your string guides, if needed, to judge the thickness.

8 **Install and level the form boards** to the string guides you set between your corner stakes.

11 **Use a mechanical tamper** to consolidate and compact the gravel base for the pour.

12 **Cut welded-wire reinforcing mesh** to fit inside the forms. Then roll it into place over the gravel.

SLOPING SLABS FOR DRAINAGE

Large exposed slabs should slope up to ¼ inch per foot to encourage drainage and eliminate puddling. One option is to slope the entire slab in one direction—for example, from the house toward the yard. Another is to crown the slab by creating curved screed boards as shown at right. Even a ½-inch crown over a 10-foot slab or driveway will encourage water flow.

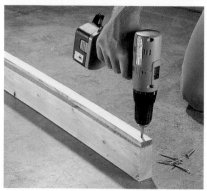

Tack a ½-in. spacer in the center, and fasten a 1x2 over it.

Following the curved screed creates a drainage slope in the pour.

13 **Fill the forms with concrete.** The wire mesh can rest on supports, or you can raise it by hand.

14 **Work a straight 2x4** in a back-and-forth motion across the forms to smooth and level the mix.

17 **Use a jointing trowel** against a straightedge to cut control joints about every 10 ft.

18 **Run an edging trowel** around the perimeter to provide a clean, crack-resistant edge.

SETTING PERMANENT FORMS

On large exposed slabs that are difficult to level and finish, you can install permanent intermediate forms that divide the pour into smaller, more manageable sections. To attach the intermediate boards, make square cuts and fasten the boards to the perimeter forms with screws. Brace the boards with stakes, but recess them so that they will not interfere with screeding.

Set intermediate forms flush with the permanent perimeter forms.

Brace intermediate forms with stakes set below the top edges.

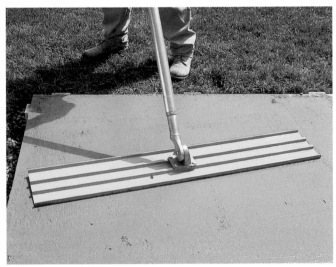

15 **Rent a bull float** with a long handle to create a smooth finish on the surface of the slab.

16 **Lightly sweep the concrete** with a broom to create a rougher, more slip-resistant surface.

19 **Cover the wet slab** with burlap (or plastic) to contain moisture. Or you can use a curing agent.

20 **Periodically spray water on the burlap** over the next several days to help the concrete cure.

When doors are anywhere from several inches to several feet off the ground, you need a landing and steps to make safe and smooth transitions in and out of the house. (Check local codes for minimum landing sizes at entries, and for riser and tread regulations.) On new homes, concrete landings and steps sometimes are included as part of the foundation, and poured at the same time. This can prevent the chronic problem of cracking where the house foundation meets the steps. But in this add-on installation you'll see how to build sturdy steps that won't shift, and how to join the structure to the house with an isolation joint. You can minimize the concrete needed on a project like this by stacking masonry rubble inside the forms. But keep the pile at least 6 inches away from all exterior surfaces to avoid weakening the pour.

Landing and Steps

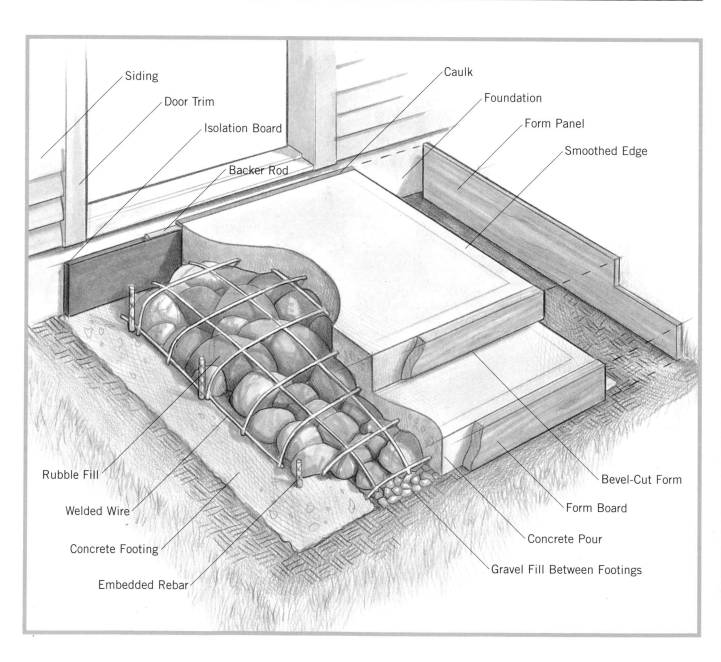

Siding
Door Trim
Isolation Board
Backer Rod
Caulk
Foundation
Form Panel
Smoothed Edge
Rubble Fill
Welded Wire
Concrete Footing
Embedded Rebar
Bevel-Cut Form
Form Board
Concrete Pour
Gravel Fill Between Footings

Landing and Steps Installation

TOOLS

- Work gloves
- Stakes and layout string
- Shovel or spade and tamper
- Square, measuring tape, pencil
- Circular saw
- Hammer and level
- Power drill-driver
- Caulking gun
- Edging trowel
- Roller (for curing sealer)

MATERIALS

- Rebar
- Concrete
- Wire lath
- ¾-in. exterior-grade plywood
- Isolation board
- 2x2 and 1x4 braces
- 1x6 riser form boards
- Clean masonry rubble
- Curing sealer (or plastic)
- 2x4 screed

SMART JOB TIP

You can add strength to the structure by adding both reinforcing wire and rebar. Rebar set into the footings helps to anchor the pour. A blanket of welded wire will help hold the rubble core in place as you pour. Setting additional rebar into the rubble core helps to tie the two masonry components together as the concrete hardens.

1 *Set up stakes and strings* to level out from the house, and then measure the rise and run of the steps.

2 *Dig two footing trenches* (below the frost line) along the sides of the landing and steps.

3 *Set rebar into the footings,* but keep them a few inches below the final concrete surface.

4 *Fill in the remaining area* with gravel, and compact it to keep the concrete from settling.

BUILT-IN DRAINS FOR LARGE LANDINGS

Drains are normally set underground to carry off water. But concrete surfaces, particularly large landings, may need drainage as well. To give rainwater a place to go, form a channel in the surface concrete and insert segmented drain fittings. Water enters through a grille and drains to an outlet pipe. You'll need to include a pipe outlet in the form before pouring.

Set prefab surface drains in a channel formed in the concrete.

Connect drainpipes to a collar at the end of the drainage channel.

5 **Transfer tread and riser dimensions** to the two side forms made of ¾-in. exterior-grade plywood.

6 **Use a circular saw** to cut out the side forms. On most jobs you'll get all the forms from one sheet.

9 **With this setup,** two braces hold the form at the nailer, and a third holds the step section.

10 **Bevel the bottom edge** of the riser form board so that you can work concrete across the step.

SLIP-RESISTANT FINISHES FOR LANDINGS AND STEPS

Concrete is normally floated to a smooth finish. This looks good, of course, but on a landing and steps a smooth surface can be dangerous, particularly in northern climates. You can create a rougher surface by embedding aggregate in the concrete before it cures or simply by brushing the surface with a stiff broom to create a striated, more slip-resistant finish.

Add exposed aggregate to the concrete before it hardens.

Broom a textured surface into the floated concrete.

7 **Tack 2x2 nailers against the foundation** ¾ in. outside the location of the side forms.

8 **Add 2x2 nailers** to the outsides of the forms, and screw them into place with angled braces.

11 **Secure the riser forms** with the bevels down. Without a bevel, the form would block the tread.

12 **Add vertical nailers** (left long) to the riser forms, and secure them to a stake with an angled 1x4.

SHARP VS. ROUNDED EDGES

Edging a landing and steps can save you repair work later on. Using a round-over edging trowel actually helps in two ways. (See step 18.) First, it allows for a clean release of the form boards. Second, it creates stronger edges that resist cracking and chipping. Sharp corners are weaker because there is less concrete for support the closer you move to the edge.

Sharp, right-angle edges can easily chip, particularly on steps.

Smooth, rounded-over edges have more strength to resist chipping.

13 *Use adhesive to fasten a piece of ½-in. isolation board against the house foundation wall.*

14 *Conserve concrete and mixing time by piling clean masonry rubble in the center of the forms.*

17 *Use a long, straight 2x4 to screed the surface, working the board back and forth on the forms.*

18 *Strengthen and finish edges of the landing and steps by running an edger just inside the forms.*

BUILDING AN ISOLATION JOINT

This joint isolates the landing from the house foundation, acts as a buffer, and prevents one from moving against and cracking the other. Mount asphalt-impregnated isolation board against the foundation, recessing the top edge down about an inch. Fill this gap with a spacer board to keep out concrete. Finish the gap with backer rod and exterior-grade caulk.

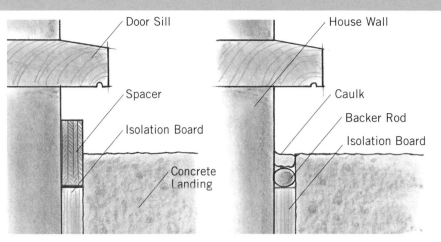

Door Sill
Spacer
Isolation Board
Concrete Landing

House Wall
Caulk
Backer Rod
Isolation Board

15 *Cover the masonry rubble* with welded wire reinforcement folded down and around the pile.

16 *Mix enough concrete* (or order ready-mix) to fill the forms at least 6 in. deep around the core.

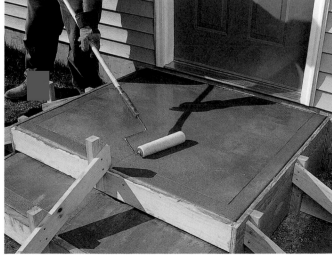

19 *The easiest way to hold in moisture* required for curing is to spray or roll on a curing sealer.

20 *Wait several days* before stripping the forms. Backing out screws is easier than pulling nails.

Concrete
Gallery

Concrete is the backbone of residential construction, providing footings, foundations, and slabs. But you can form the rugged material into elegant walls, steps, ponds, and pools, as well as walkways and driveways. You can also build in curves, imprint patterns on the surface, and add color.

Concrete's durability makes it a popular choice in swimming pool construction (opposite). It also conforms well to custom designs.

◤

Form concrete steps (right) to suit the overall design you are trying to achieve. Rounded treads make a distinctive design statement.

◤

Patios and steps (below left) gain durability and strength from a concrete slab.

◤

An eye-catching design is a creative way to enhance any environment. A zig-zagging pattern (below right) adds architectural interest.

Concrete walls (opposite) mark the entrance to a tropical garden and support the iron gates and fence around this residence.

If your design calls for festive flair (above left), concrete might be the best option. You can form concrete into curves and apply a variety of finishes.

Form concrete to join an existing landscape. A patio (above right) is transformed with the introduction of a concrete design.

Concrete is a perfect choice for walls that will be in constant contact with water (right); this only makes the concrete harder.

Block

Materials

Setting

Maintenance and Repair

Projects

CHAPTER **4**

Materials

There are many types of blocks (sometimes called concrete masonry units, or CMUs), ranging from open-faced decorative units used in screen walls to the basic concrete block used on house foundations. Generally, blocks consist of an outside shell with a hollow center that is divided by two or three vertical webs. The ends of a unit may have flanges that accept mortar and join with the adjacent block (except blocks intended for corners and the ends of walls).

Standard blocks have a face size of $7\frac{5}{8}$ inches by $15\frac{5}{8}$ inches. When you add the thickness of a standard $\frac{3}{8}$-inch mortar joint, the block measures 8 by 16 inches—its nominal size. The most commonly used block thickness is also nominally 8 inches ($7\frac{5}{8}$ inches actual dimension), but you can get nominal 4-, 6-, 10-, and 12-inch thicknesses, too.

The basic concrete block unit is called a stretcher. Stretchers are cored with two or three holes to reduce the weight as much as possible. If your project will incorporate vertical reinforcing steel (rebar) in the cores, the wall will be easier to build using special two-core units with open ends. If these units, called A-blocks, are not available, you can make your own by cutting out the ends of regular units. This will let you place blocks around rebar rather than lifting and threading them over the top of the steel.

Consider your many options when designing a concrete block wall. Some concrete blocks are gray and have flat faces with a texture that may range from coarse to relatively fine. Other blocks are more decorative and come in a variety of colors and textures. Many manufacturers also produce blocks that look like natural stone, as well as blocks with ribs, raised geometric patterns, and smooth-ground faces.

There are also several specialty blocks, such as units molded with open faces that provide some privacy without blocking out a breeze. There are also many types of interlocking blocks that you can use to build retaining walls. Most interlocking systems are installed without mortar, using connecting pins or a built-in locking channel.

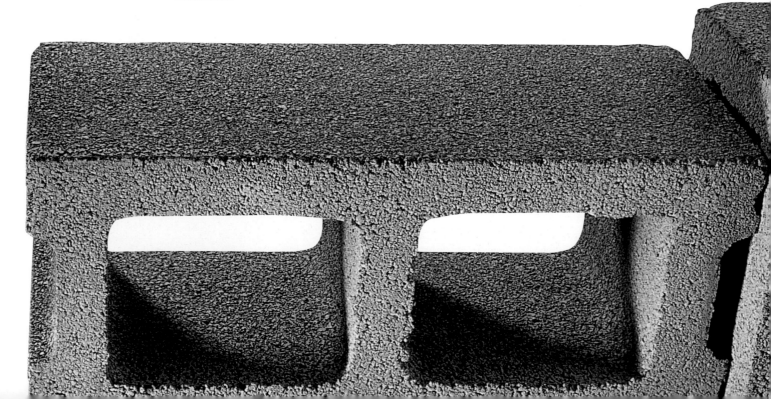

Common Block Types

Stretchers *have end flanges that butt in a mortar joint.*

End blocks *have at least one finished end.*

Cap blocks *finish off the tops of block walls.*

Rough-face blocks *offer a textured, stonelike surface.*

Interlocking blocks *for retaining walls join without mortar.*

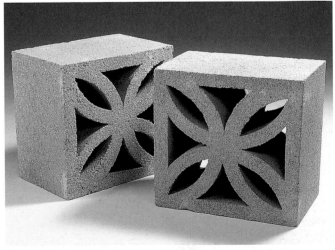

Decorative blocks *have webs on the vertical faces.*

Mixing Mortar

To maintain consistency from batch to batch, always use a container for measuring ingredients so that the proportional volume of materials remains the same. If you can't store materials close to where you'll be working, mix them in a wheelbarrow so that you can move the mortar easily. When using a mortar box, make sure it is level so that water won't collect in one end or in a corner.

First measure all dry ingredients and mix them thoroughly with a mason's hoe. If you put half the sand in first, then the cement and lime, and then add the rest of the sand, blending will be a little quicker and easier. Pull and push the materials back and forth until the color is even. Then push the mix to one end of the box or wheelbarrow, or make a hole in the middle.

Pour water into the empty end of the mixing box or the hole in the middle of the mortar mix (two gallons is about the right amount for one bag of portland cement and one bag of lime, plus sand). Mix the dry ingredients with the water, pushing and pulling the mix back and forth with a chopping motion until the consistency is uniform. About 2½ hours after the initial mixing (sooner on warm, dry days), mortar begins to harden and must be discarded.

MAKING HOLES FOR FASTENERS IN BLOCK

Working by hand, you can use a star drill and hammer, rotating the crossed tip of the tool with each blow (right). However, a standard ¼-inch drill will handle most drilling and fastening jobs in block. With a drill, use a masonry bit that has a wide carbide tip to do most of the cutting (below left). For maximum production, use a hammer drill. It has a cam that drives the bit back and forth into the masonry with a hammering action as it rotates. With either type of drill, you'll probably need to withdraw the bit once or twice to clear the buildup of block dust. Remember to wear eye protection when drilling in masonry.

HAMMER AND STAR DRILL

MASONRY BIT AND DRILL

MASONRY BIT AND HAMMER DRILL

BLOCK ESTIMATES AND MORTAR TYPES

For standard 8 x 8 x 16-inch concrete block, calculate 113 blocks per 100 square feet of wall area and add about 10 percent for breakage. For mortar, figure about 8.5 cubic feet per 100 square feet of wall area. A contractor would order the components separately and make the mix on site, but to keep your proportions consistent, buy premixed mortar.

Type M	A high-strength mortar for masonry walls that are below grade, and walls subject to high lateral or compressive loads or severe frost heaving.
Type S	A medium-high-strength mortar for walls that require strength to resist high lateral loads.
Type N	A medium-strength mortar for most masonry work that is above grade.
Type O	A low-strength mortar for interior nonbearing partitions.
Type K	Low-strength lime-sand mortar used for tuck pointing.

Masonry in various block forms can serve as durable flooring and siding; and even as translucent glass block walls.

Surface-Bond Masonry

This unorthodox building system uses a standard concrete block set in a standard running bond pattern but without any mortar in the joints. (Only the first course is laid in mortar on the footing.) Although local building departments are not likely to approve this method for foundation walls, do-it-yourselfers can use it for free-standing garden walls of moderate height.

This system is based on a combination of properties. Most important is that block has great compressive strength, which means you can stack course after course without overloading or damaging the first course. But block walls without mortar do not have much resistance to lateral (sideways) forces. To stiffen the mortarless wall, blocks need to be covered on all exposed surfaces with a ⅛-inch-thick layer of fiberglass-reinforced cement. You can't use standard cement mixes or stucco.

The finished appearance is that of a stucco wall. There is no way to see beneath the coated surfaces that the joints are not filled with mortar.

The basic sequence (shown below) is to stack the block carefully, checking for plumb and ensuring a flat face by laying blocks to a string line. Then dampen the block and trowel on the surface-bond cement.

Installing Surface-Bond Blocks

TOOLS
- Chalk line
- Mason's string and blocks
- 4-foot level
- Hose with spray head
- Trowel and hawk

MATERIALS
- Prepared concrete footing
- Concrete block
- Surface-bond cement

1 *Snap square chalk lines* on a poured concrete footing to mark the outline of the block wall.

4 *Regularly check the wall face* with a level, and shift blocks into alignment as needed.

5 *Dampen the wall* to prevent the dry block from siphoning excessive water out of the bond mix.

There is no visible way to detect that these smooth-surfaced, surface-bond walls are built without mortar joints.

2 **Stack concrete block** in a running bond pattern without any mortar in the joints.

3 **Build up the corners first,** and then use mason's blocks and string to align blocks in the courses.

6 **Apply the surface-bond mix** with upward strokes. Mix it carefully to manufacturer's instructions.

7 **Use a clean trowel** in light, sweeping strokes to smooth out the ⅛-in.-thick surface layer.

Glass Block

Building walls with blocks of glass may sound like a strange idea, but modern glass blocks are rugged enough to make large walls that let in light and keep out the weather. Interior partitions or half-walls of glass block can create rooms within rooms, defining spaces in a house without isolating them from one another. Glass block is also a popular material for custom shower enclosures and partitions in bathrooms.

Glass block is traditionally installed like concrete block with solid mortar joints. However, good glass block work is a specialized skill, more so than laying block or brick, and it is nor-mally a job for a mason. Generally, large projects are laid only a few courses at a time. This is necessary to prevent the weight of many courses from compressing the mortar in lower courses.

Some blocks are designed to make installation more suitable for do-it-yourselfers. Glass-block kits with clear plastic spacers are stacked and sealed with silicone caulk instead of mortar. Other kits offer blocks that snap into a metal framework and glass-like blocks made of plastic that clip together with interlocking flanges. You can also buy prefabricated glass-block window units, which you can install in a rough opening like a standard window.

Glass block offers privacy and security as well as decorative details, such as curved corner block.

Installing Kit-Form Glass Block

TOOLS
- Drill or screwdriver
- Level
- Measuring tape

MATERIALS
- Glass block kit, including track and spacers

1 *In a typical kit,* a structural channel screwed to the framing conceals the glass-block edges.

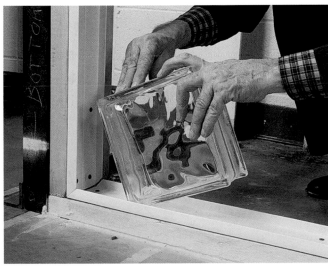

2 *Overall framing dimensions* need to account for the width of the blocks, tracks, and spacers.

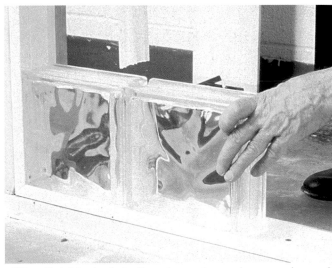

3 *Set blocks into the channels,* and use a piece of the flexible gasket material to check spacing.

4 *Set a full length of the gasket* over a full course. The gasket is molded to fit into block ridges.

5 *Set spacer gaskets in all seams,* and caulk exposed seams that are normally grouted.

CHAPTER 4 **Block**

Setting Block

Although building with masonry block is easier for do-it-yourselfers than pouring large walls of concrete, the work can be taxing. Standard concrete blocks weigh about 40 pounds each. It's difficult enough to lift one of the heavy blocks up into position, but even tougher when you have to lower it gingerly onto a bed of mortar.

Installation Sequence

Pros build up the corners, called leads, before filling in the blocks along each course. The first course of a corner should be three units long. The rest are set back one-half block in each course. This establishes a running bond pattern in which the units of one course are offset one-half block from the courses above and below.

To start, use enough mortar to make a bed that is ½ to ¾ inch thick, slightly wider than a block, and at least three blocks long. Lay the corner or end unit first, pressing it firmly down into the mortar. Measure to make sure the resulting mortar bed is about ⅜ inch high, and tap the unit lightly with the trowel handle if necessary. Use a 4-foot level to check for level and plumb.

As you add blocks, butter the head joints by

Setting Block

TOOLS
- Mixing tub or wheelbarrow
- Trowel and hawk
- Level
- Striking tool

MATERIALS
- Mortar
- Block

1 *Embed the first course* in a liberal amount of mortar that contacts all of the bottom surfaces.

3 *Masons often build corners* several courses high and then fill in with blocks to a string guide.

4 *Place mortar on the block webs* by striking your trowel on the block so that the mortar slides off.

standing the units on end and swiping mortar onto the flanges with the edge of the trowel. Lift the block by the ends, and place it gently onto the mortar bed and firmly against the adjacent block. Mortar should ooze from both the head and bed joints. Remove the excess mortar from the face of the blocks with the trowel blade.

Aside fom the first course, blocks are laid with face-shell bedding. (The 8 x 16-inch outside surfaces of a concrete block are called the face shells.) Place mortar along the top of the face shells, which are about 1½ inches wide. Build the wall by filling in between leads. Then start over with new leads built higher and higher.

Filling In Between Leads

Stretch a line to mark the top of each course as you build up the wall. Check the line with a line level, and use line blocks to hold the string about ⅟₁₆ inch away from the face of the wall.

Fill in the first course between leads, buttering the flanges as you lay blocks and checking the tops of the blocks with a 4-foot level to make sure that each course is aligned. Check the blocks with a level to make sure that they are plumb, and use the side of the level as a straightedge to align the faces of the units in each course.

The last block to place is called the closure block. You should have just enough space left

2 *Tap the block* into position with the heel of your trowel, checking progress with a level.

5 *Finish an exterior wall* by embedding cap blocks (sold in 2-in. and 4-in. thicknesses) in mortar.

INSTALLING SILLS ON BLOCK

Measure from the outside of the wall to find the location of the bolts. Then drill a hole somewhat larger than the bolt diameters. Set the sill onto the foam sealer with the anchor bolts protruding. Slip a large washer on each one, and then tighten the nuts.

for this block plus a head joint on each end. To make sure you get full head joints, butter the ends of the adjacent blocks and both ends of the closure block. Lower the block into place from above, being careful not to dislodge the adjacent blocks.

As you lay the concrete blocks, remove excess mortar from the face of the joints with the edge of the trowel. After the mortar has begun to cure, tool the joints to compress the mortar and decrease moisture absorption. The joints are ready for tooling when the mortar is thumbprint hard, meaning that you can press your thumb against the mortar and leave a print impression without the mortar sticking to your thumb.

Use a rounded jointing tool to make concave joints. Check the mortar frequently, and tool the joints a few at a time when the surface is just the right consistency. As the joints are tooled, small pieces of mortar, called tailings, will be squeezed out at the edges of the joints. Remove them with the edge of the trowel.

After laying the closure block and confirming that the course is level and plumb, you can build up the wall quickly. Once you're comfortable with the process, set three or four blocks on end, mortar their flanges, mortar the bed joint, and lay a number of blocks in rapid succession.

CUTTING BLOCK

On many projects you can get by with store-bought, preformed half-sized blocks. These are designed to create staggered joints in courses. But there may be times when you need to cut a slightly smaller or larger partial block. Concrete block, like all other types of masonry, often does not break smoothly. It helps if you use a circular saw with a special masonry-cutting blade (right). But the expensive blades can wear down quickly. Working by hand, you can score blocks on both sides with a brick set (below left). You may have to deepen the score to get a clean break as you strike along the lines (below right) to break the block.

CUTTING WITH MASONRY BLADE

SCORING WITH BRICK SET

CUTTING WITH BRICK SET

THREE WAYS TO STRENGTHEN BLOCK WALLS

FILL VOIDS

Lay wire mesh under the top course of block to hold back mortar, allowing you to fill the upper voids.

Filling the upper voids strengthens the wall and seals the voids, which may be required by code.

SET REBAR

Voids will align even though courses of blocks are staggered, leaving a clear vertical space for rebar.

Vertical rebar (generally placed 4 ft. on center in foundation walls) extends from footing to sill.

EMBED Z-STRIP

Spread a bed of mortar across all surfaces to support horizontal joint reinforcement.

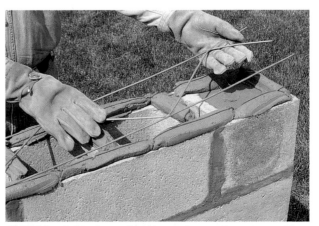

Embed reinforcing wire in mortar under every other course and under the top course.

Maintenance and Repair

To keep basement moisture and leaks from turning into major problems, inspect basement walls on a regular basis, especially after heavy rains. In addition to checking for cracks and holes, look for moisture penetration through the mortar joints in concrete blocks and floor-to-wall joints. Also look for gaps around windows, doors, and vents, such as dryer vents.

Repair holes and cracks as soon as you discover them, but bear in mind that filling a crack takes care of the symptom, not the underlying cause. A large amount of water entering a basement is a sign of a drainage problem that is best dealt with outside of the house—for instance, by installing an area drain.

Small to moderate-size cracks that are stable usually do not indicate a major structural problem. Larger or expanding cracks could signal a structural flaw in the wall or a drainage problem that is undermining the foundation. Either way, if the problem goes unchecked, the result could be serious damage to your house. Look for new cracks or old ones that reopen after repairs, and monitor them (as shown at top right) to determine whether they are stable or active.

Filling Cracks and Holes

To patch a small crack, sweep out any loose debris and fill with cement. Fill any cracks that become wet with hydraulic cement or two-part epoxy filler. Hydraulic cement is easy to work with, can be used even on active leaks, and swells as it hardens to fill irregular voids.

A good procedure is to enlarge and undercut the crack with a hammer and a cold chisel. (Undercutting helps to hold the filler in place.) Then brush the crack clean and moisten it. Use a trowel to apply hydraulic cement or epoxy, smooth the surface, and then allow the filler to dry.

To fill a hole, shape a handful of hydraulic cement into a cone, squeeze the point into the hole, and hold it in place for several minutes until the cement hardens. Once you have made the repairs, you can refinish the patches (and the entire wall) with masonry surfacer or sealer.

DIAGNOSING CRACKS

Minor cracks in block walls generally are nothing to worry about as long as the cracks are stable. (You'll often see debris or old paint in stable cracks.) Larger cracks that appear suddenly or keep expanding could signal a serious structural flaw, particularly if the crack extends in a staircase pattern through several courses. To track a new crack, tape gridded tracing paper over the area, outline the crack, and measure its length and widest parts. Mark the corners of the tracing paper on the wall so that you can reposition it exactly in order to see if the crack changes over time.

Finishing Rough Block Walls

TOOLS

- Hammer and cold chisel
- Wire brush and sponge
- Trowel
- Striking tool

MATERIALS

- Cleaning solution (or soap and water)
- Patching mortar
- Masonry surfacer paint

3 *Use a trowel to fill joints* with mortar where they have been left rough by the builder.

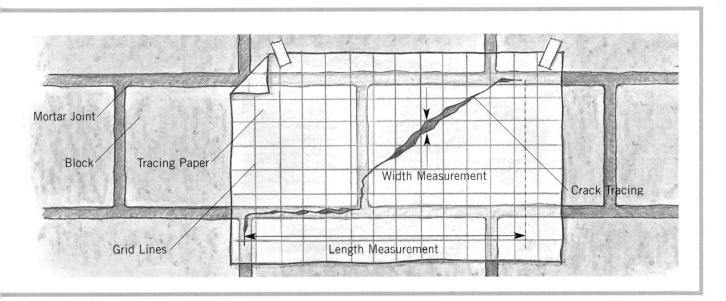

Mortar Joint

Block   Tracing Paper

Width Measurement

Crack Tracing

Grid Lines

Length Measurement

1 *Use a 2-lb. masonry hammer* and cold chisel to chip off excess mortar protruding from seams.

2 *Wash and rinse the block wall* to get the best adhesion from a masonry-surfacer paint.

4 *Use a stiff brush* to apply a prime coat of masonry surfacer to patched areas and seams.

5 *Use a roller* fitted with a long-napped sleeve to work the surfacer into the rough-faced block.

Cleaning Masonry Block

There are several ways to clean masonry. Most of the methods apply to brick, concrete, and stone as well as to block. Many of the more complicated methods are generally handled by contractors, including sandblasting and cleaning with chemicals or steam. Another option, cleaning with a pressure-washer, is a job that most do-it-yourselfers can handle.

Sandblasting takes away surface and embedded dirt. Chemical- and steam-cleaning contractors can solve a variety of problems, including removing efflorescence, which is a powdery crust. (See "How Efflorescence Forms," page 99.)

When vines start growing into cracks in mortar joints, you should cut the roots as close to the wall as possible and treat the ends with ammonium phosphate paste to kill the plant.

Mold and mildew also may take hold on masonry that is not exposed to sunlight. To test a discolored patch of block wall, drop a small amount of bleach on the spot. The bleach will whiten mildew growth but will have no effect on dirt. To clear the mildew, scrub the area with a solution of one part bleach to one part warm water, and then rinse.

Remove stains from iron hardware by applying a solution of oxalic acid. Mix about 1 pound of the crystals in a gallon of water with ½ pound of ammonium bifluoride, brush the mix over the stained area, and then rinse.

Patching Small Holes

TOOLS
- Hammer and cold chisel
- Trowel
- Scraper blades or hawk

MATERIALS
- Patching mortar

2 **Brush away dirt and dust.** *Hold patching mortar against the wall, and then force it into the hole.*

Replacing Broken Block

TOOLS
- Hammer and cold chisel
- Drill and masonry bit
- Wire brush
- Trowel
- Striking tool

MATERIALS
- Mortar
- Replacement block

1 **For many repairs,** *you only need to remove the damaged block face. To start, drill a series of holes.*

1 *To make patch material bond securely* to the block, chip away cracked edges with a cold chisel.

3 *Smooth out small patches* by running the side of a mason's trowel over the block face.

HOW EFFLORESCENCE FORMS

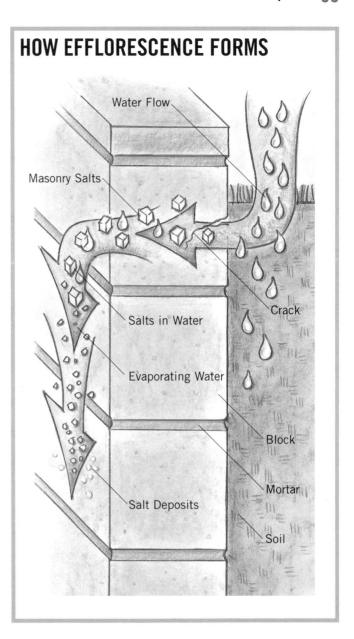

Water Flow

Masonry Salts

Salts in Water

Crack

Evaporating Water

Block

Mortar

Salt Deposits

Soil

2 *Chip away the interior webs,* and then butter the edges of a split replacement block.

3 *Support the replacement* with a wedge while you force mortar deep into joints before tooling.

Drying Out Basements

Water can leak into basements through cracks or mortar joints in the foundation walls. But there is another common cause of basement moisture: condensation, which forms when water vapor in warm air hits the cool foundation walls.

Leaks can usually be identified by sight and repaired with hydraulic cement. This dense patch material swells as it hardens and can be used on wet cracks and active leaks. The foil test shown below will help you decide whether moisture is due to a leak or condensation.

Solve condensation problems by improving ventilation and using air conditioners and dehumidifiers. Eliminating seepage, however, is another matter. If seepage occurs only during heavy rains, the solution could be as simple as extending a downspout so that the runoff is directed farther away from foundation walls or regrading the soil so that it slopes away from the foundation.

Correct minor seepage from the inside by coating foundation walls with a masonry sealer (either a cement- or tar-based product or a waterproof silicone sealer). As a last (and very expensive) resort, you may need to re-excavate the foundation down to the footings to install perimeter drains and to apply new waterproofing.

FOIL TEST FOR WET BASEMENTS

Water leaking through a crack in a foundation is usually easy to detect. But basement walls also can become wet due to excessive moisture in the air that condenses on the masonry, particularly in the summer. To determine whether you have a leak or a condensation problem, tape down a patch of aluminum foil, which moisture can't penetrate, over a section of clean, dry wall (right). Check for moisture after 48 hours. If the foil surface is wet but the wall below it is dry (lower left), the problem is condensation. If the foil surface is dry but the wall beneath it is wet (lower right), then the problem is water seeping through the wall.

FOIL TEST PATCH

CONDENSATION: FOIL WET—WALL DRY

LEAK: FOIL DRY—WALL WET

Repairing and Sealing Basement Block

TOOLS
- Scraper
- Patching trowel
- Hammer and cold chisel
- Jointing tool
- Caulking gun

MATERIALS
- Cement mix (or hydraulic cement)
- Elastomeric caulk

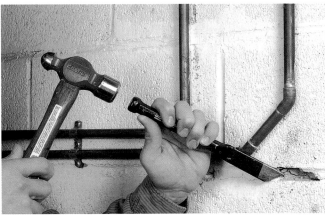

1 *To repair a leaking joint,* start by chipping out any loose mortar and sweeping away debris.

2 *Fill a dry seam* with fresh mortar, but use hydraulic cement to fill over an active leak.

3 *Before the cement hardens,* use a jointing tool (or any curved tool) to smooth out the seam.

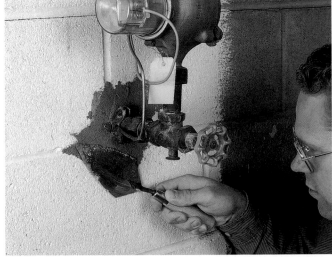

4 *Seal holes* where pipes extend through the foundation by filling the broken-out area with cement.

5 *Seal small cracks* at the floor with an elastomeric joint sealant or a hydraulic cement patch.

alls made of concrete block are fundamental components of many buildings.
You can use them to build the foundation
of a house, a retaining wall with weep hole, or a
privacy wall in the garden. This project shows
the step-by-step fundamentals of construction
you can apply in many situations—even using
blocks to build yourself a barbecue. Where the
walls bear weight, as in a foundation, you'll need
to check local building codes that regulate features such as the size of the footing and the
amount of metal reinforcement required in the
wall. Different situations also call for different
finishing details, such as waterproofing on a
foundation or stucco on an exposed wall. You'll
cap some walls with block or stone and others
with a wooden sill plate. Yet the construction of
mortared blocks is generally the same.

Block Wall

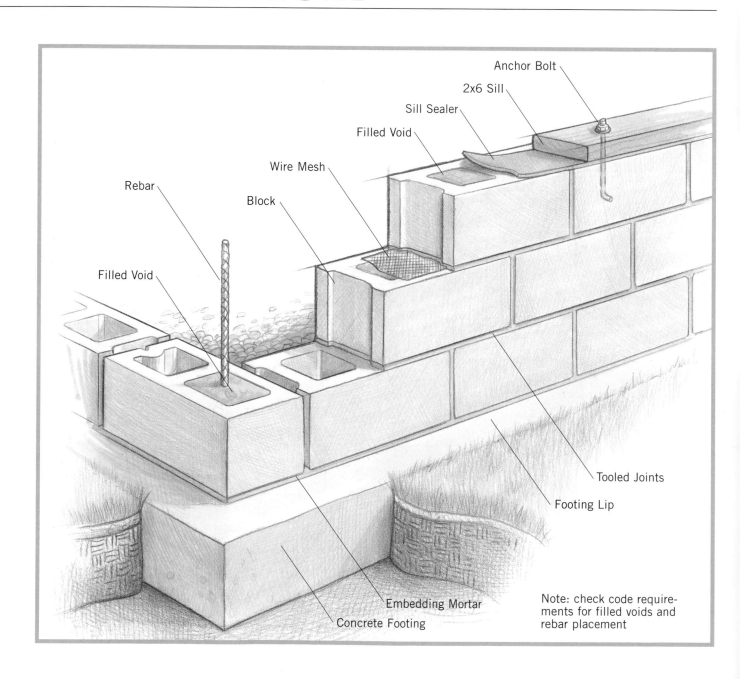

Anchor Bolt
2x6 Sill
Sill Sealer
Filled Void
Wire Mesh
Rebar
Block
Filled Void
Tooled Joints
Footing Lip
Embedding Mortar
Concrete Footing

Note: check code require-
ments for filled voids and
rebar placement

Block Wall Installation

TOOLS

- Work gloves and safety glasses
- Pencil
- Shovels and tamper
- Levels
- Mason's blocks and string
- Hammer and brick set
- Trowels and striking tool
- Wheelbarrow or mixer
- Bucket

MATERIALS

- Concrete blocks
- Mortar
- Wire lath
- Rebar (some walls)
- Anchor bolts (some walls)
- Concrete and gravel
  (for block wall footing)

SMART JOB TIP

Block walls that bear weight or need extra resistance to tipping can be reinforced. You'll need to check local codes on load-bearing foundations. You may need to insert vertical rebar into voids, coupling it to rebar in the footing. A zigzag assembly of wires can reinforce the blocks horizontally.

CHAPTER 4 Block

1 *Lay the first course* of block without mortar in order to plan the layout and mark the corner joints.

2 *Lay a row of mounded mortar* to form an embedding layer for the edges and webs of the first course.

3 *Lay the first block* in the mortar bed; check your marks; and tap the block into level position.

4 *Set another block* on the opposite corner. Attach a string as a guideline using mason's blocks.

CUTTING BLOCK

The traditional method for breaking block is to score the surfaces with a brick set, tapping lightly, and then strike sharply on the score line. On large projects you may want to speed up the process by using a circular saw with a special masonry-cutting blade. With both methods, be sure to wear gloves and safety glasses to guard against flying chips of masonry.

Cut by hand using a wide-faced brick set and 2-lb. hammer.

Reinforced masonry blades cut quickly but wear out fast.

5 **Butter the blocks** by placing mortar on the end of each flange with a tap of your trowel.

6 **Shape the mortar on each flange** into a U-shape by swiping the sides with your trowel.

9 **Set the block** in correct alignment, rather than trying to slide it into position, dislodging the mortar.

10 **Set up a string guide** from a nail that is embedded temporarily in mortar under the block.

CONTROL JOINTS

The Michigan joint is one type of control joint in long walls that prevents cracking. Although cracks occur there, they are hidden in the continuous joint. The combination of felt paper and a core filled with mortar provides lateral strength in the wall, even though the joints in courses are aligned. To make the joints continuous, you need to add half blocks in alternate courses.

Use felt paper to keep the mortar from bonding to one of the blocks.

Fill the open joints with a bead of flexible, exterior-grade caulk.

7 **Work in from the wall ends,** aligning each block face at the same distance relative to the string.

8 **Mortar all the internal webs** when installing wire reinforcing strips, which tie corners together.

11 **Check corner blocks** for plumb on both sides of the corner before setting new guide strings.

12 **As you fill in along the string,** be sure to check the edge using a level or any other straightedge.

CHAPTER 4 **Block**

FOOTINGS AND FOUNDATIONS

A load-bearing block foundation wall generally rests on a reinforced footing at least 8 inches thick and twice as wide as the blocks. On top of the wall, voids in the blocks are filled and anchor bolts are embedded, with the threaded ends protruding about 2 inches. The bolts, spaced 4 to 6 feet on center and 12 inches from the ends of boards, serve to hold down the building's sill plate.

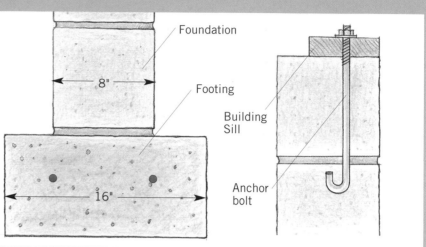

Foundation

Footing

Building Sill

Anchor bolt

13 *Work to a level string* set with a line level, and periodically double-check with a spirit level.

14 *If you build up corners* before filling-in blocks on courses, their top edges should align.

17 *Install wire lath* in the next-to-last course to support mortar filling the top-course voids.

18 *Fill the voids* in the top course to seal the wall. Foundations may also need rebar and anchors.

CAPPING BLOCK WALLS

There are many ways to cap a free-standing block wall. The standard treatment is to apply a full bedding layer of mortar and set concrete cap blocks, finished on all sides. You can instead set wide trim blocks to form an overhang, decorative blocks with see-through webs, or stones—either large cut pieces or a series of smaller stones set in a mortar bed.

You can finish the wall with cap blocks set in a bed of mortar.

Instead, you can set pieces of stone into a full bed of mortar.

15 **Use a trowel** to remove excess mortar squeezed out of the joints by the weight of the block.

16 **Use a jointing tool** before the mortar sets to smooth and slightly recess the joints.

19 **Embed anchor bolts** in the filled block voids. The bolts will secure wooden sill plates.

20 **Bolts must protrude** at least 2 in. to reach through a 2x6 sill plate, washers, and nuts.

CHAPTER 4 Block

The two keys to building a sound retaining wall are the strength of its basic construction and the wall's ability to release groundwater, which is the biggest cause of deterioration and tipover. Of the many possible designs and materials, the strongest is solid masonry—either poured concrete or the block construction shown in this project. The blocks rest on a poured foundation and are reinforced with vertical rebars embedded in the concrete. There are two systems for reducing the amount of hydrostatic pressure on a wall. One is a water-collection trench filled with gravel on the high side of the wall. This employs a drainpipe near the base to carry the water to a release point at the end of the wall. The other system is a series of weep holes that allow any water reaching the wall to flow through.

Block Retaining Wall

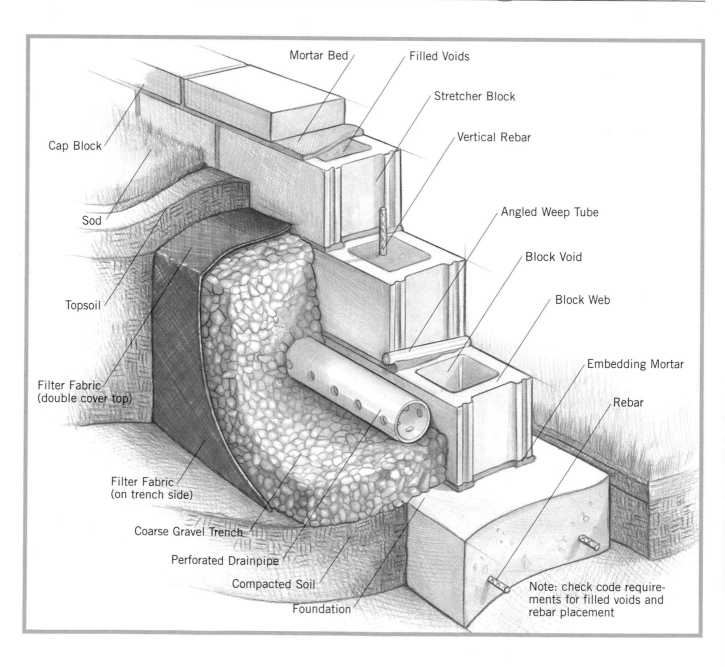

Mortar Bed

Filled Voids

Stretcher Block

Cap Block

Vertical Rebar

Sod

Angled Weep Tube

Block Void

Topsoil

Block Web

Embedding Mortar

Filter Fabric
(double cover top)

Rebar

Filter Fabric
(on trench side)

Coarse Gravel Trench

Perforated Drainpipe

Compacted Soil

Foundation

Note: check code requirements for filled voids and rebar placement

Block Retaining Wall Installation

TOOLS

- Work gloves and safety glasses
- Shovel
- Hammer
- Tamper
- Hoe
- Wheelbarrow and bucket
- Mason's trowel
- Measuring tape and pencil
- Chalk line or string guide

MATERIALS

- Wooden forms
- Concrete
- Rebar
- Mortar
- Concrete block
- Galvanized pipe
- Gravel
- Perforated drainpipe
- Filter fabric

SMART JOB TIP

With a drainage trench and pipe to carry water away from the wall, you need only small-diameter weep holes set over the first course about every two or three blocks. The small diameter minimizes trimming at block corners. Without a drainage trench, and where water flow is great, use larger pipes.

1 **Dig a trench** *to accommodate the poured concrete footing you will use to support the wall.*

2 **Construct a form** *twice as wide as the block, and brace it with stakes driven outside the form.*

3 **Mix concrete for the footing** *in a wheelbarrow, and screed across the form to level the pour.*

4 **Before the concrete hardens** *set lengths of rebar aligned with the block voids.*

CHAPTER 4 **Block**

GUARDING WEEP HOLES

The main problem with weep holes is clogging, which lets water build up pressure on the high side of the wall. A gravel trench backed and topped with filter fabric will help keep out dirt. In addition, cover the pipe inlets with galvanized wire mesh. Shape it to create a hollow area around the pipe. Then pour in gravel carefully so you don't dislodge the mesh.

Cut galvanized mesh and form it into a basket to cover the pipe.

A wire basket keeps the uphill end of the pipe from clogging.

5 *Set the block* with buttered ends into a layer of mortar. Use a string to check alignment.

6 *Form sloped weep holes* with a ¾-in. galvanized or PVC pipe set into the joint at every third block.

9 *Set solid cap blocks* on the wall, tapping them into position, and checking alignment and level.

10 *Add about 6 in. of gravel* on the high side of the wall. Note the screened weep-hole pipe.

LAYING FILTER LANDSCAPE FABRIC

Filter fabric is a tightly woven material that lets water through but filters out fine dirt that can eventually clog weep holes and the entire drainage trench. You can spread fabric over the gravel on the high side of the gravel trench behind the wall and over the filled trench, as well. The fabric cover allows you to replace topsoil and sod, and conceal the gravel.

Filter fabric lets water into the gravel but keeps out most dirt.

You can cover the filter fabric with mulch or topsoil and sod.

7 *Use a trowel to remove excess mortar that squeezes out of the joints.*

8 *For maximum strength, fill the voids between the block webs. Note the rebar.*

11 *Lay perforated pipe, holes down, with a slight slope to drain water toward the end of the wall.*

12 *Bury the pipe, and fill the trench with gravel. You can apply filter fabric and sod at the top.*

I f mortaring a masonry garden wall seems like too much work, or just too complicated, try one of the interlocking designs. Available in many sizes and finishes, these manufactured blocks are built to stack without mortar. Some have a lip to create an offset so that the wall can slope back into a hill. Others, like the units in this project, have slots to help you offset the blocks or align them in a vertical wall.

Because these blocks have no mortar joints, the structure is porous, so they can serve either in a retaining wall laid into a bank or as a freestanding garden wall. Typical interlocking systems use rigid plastic pins set both horizontally and vertically in preformed slots to keep the blocks aligned. To stagger joints, you will need to cut a few blocks. Aside from that, the job involves heavy but very simple stacking.

Interlocking Block Wall

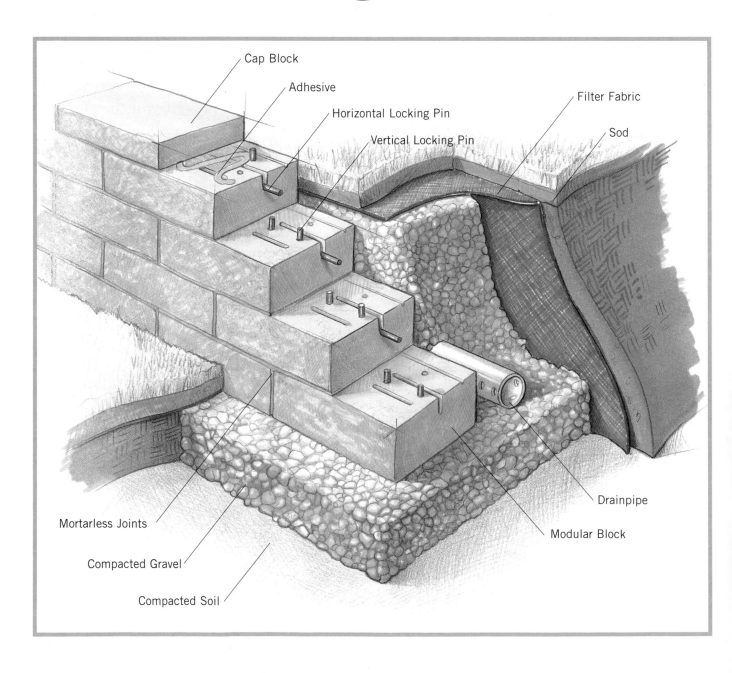

Interlocking Block Retaining Wall Installation

TOOLS
- Shovel and wheelbarrow
- 4x4 for tamping soil
- Caulking gun
- Spirit level
- Hammer and brick set
- Work gloves and safety glasses
- String and mason's blocks

MATERIALS
- Retaining wall block
- Block connectors
- Perforated pipe
- Gravel
- Adhesive for cap block

SMART JOB TIP
Generally, you can lay a short wall of interlocked blocks on compacted or undisturbed soil covered with about 6 inches of gravel. Be sure that the base course is level. Check manufacturer's recommendations about height limits and requirements for footings under higher and heavier walls.

1 **Dig a trench** for the retaining wall, leaving enough room on the high side for gravel and a drainpipe.

2 **Compact the soil** at the bottom of the shallow trench using a 4x4 or hand tamper.

3 **Fill the trench** with about 4 in. of gravel to provide a firm base for the interlocking blocks.

4 **Place the first few blocks** on the gravel bed, aligning the faces and checking the tops for level.

IMPROVING DRAINAGE

Even a porous block retaining wall may need supplemental drainage. Although a porous, unmortared wall doesn't need the extra drainage to resist cracking or tipover, it might need drainage to prevent muddy streams of water from washing through it. The best bet is a gravel trench with perforated pipe at the base, sloped slightly to carry water away from the wall.

Perforated pipe sections fit into one another behind long walls.

A wrap of filter fabric keeps out silt that can clog the pipe.

5 **Install perforated drain piping**, holes down, on gravel behind the wall after laying the first course.

6 **Set mason's blocks** at each end of the wall with a string to check the face as you insert connectors.

9 **Insert plastic pegs** in preformed holes to align the courses. Some systems allow setback positioning.

10 **Also install connectors** horizontally in preformed slots between mating blocks.

TERRACING SLOPING YARDS

Retaining walls are crucial on sloping sites where you want to terrace part of the yard to make it flat. One key to terracing is to equalize cut and fill. That means planning the retaining wall location and height so that the amount of dirt you remove, or cut, from the high side of the slope equals the amount you need to fill on the low side to make a level yard.

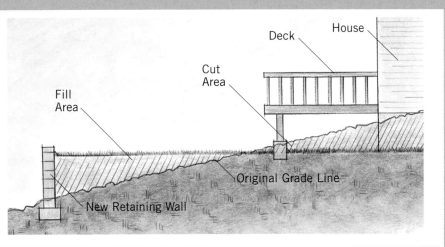

7 *Cover the perforated drainpipe* with gravel up to the height of the first course.

8 *Use a hammer and brick set* to cut half blocks for the ends so that you can stagger the block joints.

11 *Check for plumb* regularly as you work. Some types of block step back a bit in each course.

12 *Attach cap blocks* using a caulking gun and construction adhesive as specified.

This traditional masonry barbecue is one of the more complex projects for a do-it-yourselfer, mainly because it requires two types of materials and two types of walls. Building a block wall is straightforward. In this case, 4-inch block reduces the unnecessary bulk of standard 8-inch units. Building the firebrick liner wall is also a relatively easy job. The trick is to account for the different sizes so that the walls are the same height. If they aren't, you won't be able to level cap stones on the walls.

The extra wrinkle with this design is that block walls require ⅜-inch mortar joints, while firebrick walls require joints only ⅛ to ¼ inch thick. To be sure of the final heights, you should set portions of both walls in place on temporary spacers. As you build, check the heights at every course, and make minor adjustments as needed.

Barbecue

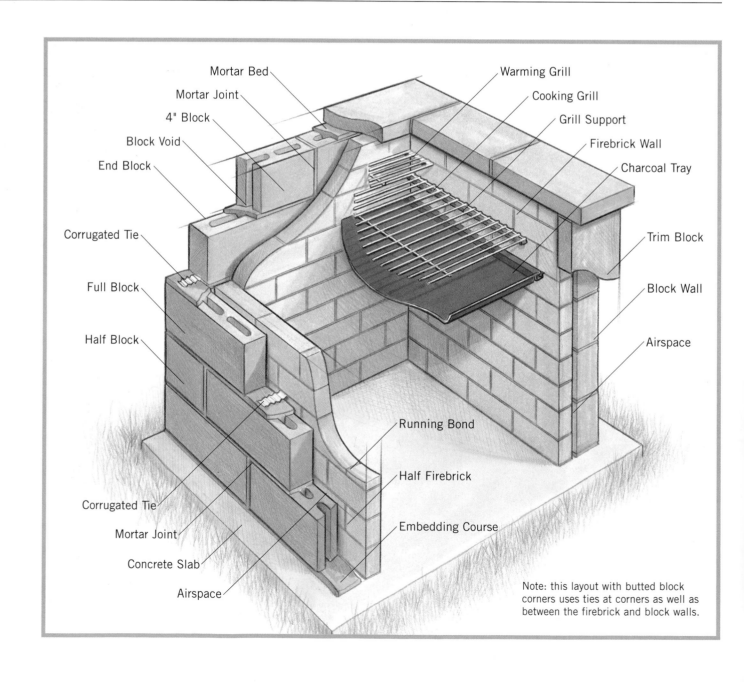

Mortar Bed
Mortar Joint
4" Block
Block Void
End Block
Corrugated Tie
Full Block
Half Block
Corrugated Tie
Mortar Joint
Concrete Slab
Airspace
Running Bond
Half Firebrick
Embedding Course
Warming Grill
Cooking Grill
Grill Support
Firebrick Wall
Charcoal Tray
Trim Block
Block Wall
Airspace

Note: this layout with butted block corners uses ties at corners as well as between the firebrick and block walls.

Barbecue Installation

TOOLS

- Work gloves
- Measuring tape
- Trowels
- Level
- Mason's blocks and string
- Hammer and brickset
- Striking tool
- Wheelbarrow or mixing tub

MATERIALS

- Concrete blocks
- Concrete cap blocks
- Firebrick
- Concrete and firebrick mortar
- Wood spacers
- Corrugated ties
- Angle irons or anchors
- Prepared concrete footing
- Charcoal pan and grills

SMART JOB TIP

The exact size of the barbecue depends on several factors, such as the dimensions of the blocks and firebricks. Another crucial factor is the size of the charcoal pan and cooking grills. You should shop around and find these units before finalizing your plan to be sure that they will fit with about ½ inch to spare from side to side.

1 ***Start by laying out*** *the outer block edges on a reinforced concrete slab or footing as required.*

2 ***Place the 4-in. blocks*** *to the line in a dry layout, and use spacers to simulate the ⅜-in. mortar joint.*

3 ***Also make a dry layout*** *with the inner layer of firebrick. The ⅛-in. joints are marked on a board.*

4 ***Spread a liberal layer of mortar*** *on the slab, and embed the first course of block.*

BUILDING A CUTTING JIG

Cutting masonry blocks is relatively easy because the blocks are heavy and stay in place as you cut. Cutting bricks is more difficult. To make the job easier and safer, build a simple cutting jig. This one has a ¾-inch plywood platform and small blocks screwed in place to hold the brick as you cut. Spaces between side blocks provide clearance for the saw blade as you cut half bricks.

Clamp the plywood platform of the jig securely before cutting.

Screwed-down blocks hold the brick as you cut half-brick units.

5 *Tap the block into position* with the heel of your trowel, and check the top of the course for level.

6 *Insert galvanized ties in mortar* wherever you cannot create interlocked layers at the corners.

9 *Use a spacer* to keep the courses of firebrick about ¾ in. away from the courses of block.

10 *Use half bricks* to create a running bond pattern of staggered joints in the firebrick.

BLOCK VERSUS FIREBRICK JOINTS

One of the trickiest parts of this project is to keep the courses in modular scale. You may need to make small adjustments as you build so that the top surfaces of brick and block will be level with each other—at least close enough to support an embedding coat of mortar and cap stones. It pays to try a vertical dry layout with spacers before building with mortar.

The standard joint for block is $\frac{3}{8}$ in. thick and easy to tool.

Joints in firebrick typically are $\frac{1}{8}$ to $\frac{1}{4}$ in. thick and harder to tool.

7 **Extend two ties** fully across the joint, and cover them with mortar before setting the next course.

8 **Tool the exterior seams** before the mortar sets up. You don't need to finish the interior seams.

11 **Secure the brick** to the block wall with galvanized ties already embedded into the block joints.

12 **As you build up the firebrick courses,** regularly check all of the wall faces with a level.

ADDING FINISHED STONE FACINGS

Rough-surfaced masonry cap blocks can form clean edges for the barbecue. But you can easily upgrade the job with a cut-stone finish on both the end faces and the top of the barbecue. This alternative design has thin stone that is easy to work with. Consider installing stone wide enough to provide a substantial overhang to serve as a handy work and storage surface.

Press the cut stone into a stiff bed of mortar on the face ends.

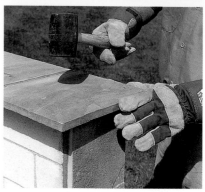

Set cap stones in mortar with an overhang on all sides of the wall.

13 *Regularly check the wall faces with a straight-edge, even if you lay them to a string line.*

14 *Embed an angle iron (or another holder) to support the charcoal and cooking grills.*

17 *Spread a full bed of mortar over the brick and block as an embedding layer for the caps.*

18 *Set cap blocks in mortar on the top and face walls, in this case, with a small overhang.*

ALTERNATIVE HOLDERS FOR GRILLS

The charcoal pan and cooking grill must be supported along the firebrick walls. The project has embedded tracks so that you can easily slide the units in and out. But you can install short lengths of protruding rebar (right) or galvanized hardware such as a T-shaped mending plate (far right). Plan ahead carefully to install the supports in courses at the right heights.

You can install rebar in drilled holes after the brick wall is built.

Install protruding plates in mortar as the brick courses are laid.

15 **Cover the embedded grill support** with firebrick mortar before adding another course.

16 **Firebrick joints are narrow** (⅛ to ¼ in.) and tooled with small implements, such as a pencil.

19 **With the mortar hardened** and the joints tooled, set the charcoal pan and cooking grill in place.

20 **This barbecue has room** to install a small warming grill on rods above the main grill.

 Block Gallery

Block is another basic building unit that comes in many forms, including glass. You can dress up standard concrete block with a stucco finish and choose from a great variety of molded units that offer textured surfaces and interlocking designs that are ideal for retaining walls.

A glass-block corridor leads into an innovative kitchen (opposite). Concrete block walls are aesthetically pleasing and avant-garde.

Interlocking blocks come in a variety of styles. A deeply textured surface gives a garage rustic charm (above left).

Concrete blocks set diagonally atop a stucco wall (above right) add a decorative touch to a tropical garden.

Glass block, available in many finishes from clear to frosted, can provide a wall of light to brighten a room (right).

A glass-block shower stall (top left) lets in natural light, offers privacy, and provides an elegant design touch.

A backsplash made of glass block (left) is an easy way to open up a kitchen.

A concrete-block wall blends seamlessly into the greenery of a lush garden (above right).

Some designs incorporate a multitude of materials. Stucco covers concrete block on this staircase (opposite above).

Modular blocks with textured surfaces (opposite below) can form finished screening and retaining walls.

Stucco

Materials

Applications

Maintenance and Repair

Projects

CHAPTER **5**

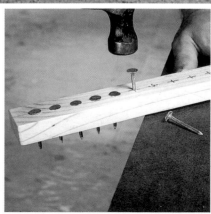

Materials

Stucco is a versatile masonry material that can be formed into almost any shape and given a variety of finish textures. Like mortar, stucco is made with portland cement, sand, and water—and sometimes lime. The term stucco applies to the entire thickness of layers, from base to surface. Stucco is applied with a steel trowel, the same trowel used in finishing concrete. A plasterer's hawk may be used to carry convenient amounts of wet stucco to the wall.

Stucco can transform an unattractive block foundation or garden wall into an attractive addition to the landscape. Stucco can also be applied to mesh that has been attached to plywood, for example when using stucco over the sheathing of a wood-framed house.

Stucco Pros & Cons

Stucco is popular because of its durability and uniquely textured appearance. However, problems can arise in this weather-resistant shell. If the house foundation sinks unevenly or new framing members shift as they dry out, the movement can create enough stress to crack the rigid stucco walls.

Problems can also arise in the stucco itself. Fresh stucco (and the masonry wall underneath) may contain salt-based compounds that can be carried to the surface. Here's how it happens. As the moisture evaporates, the salt deposits leave a residue on the surface called efflorescence. Although the alkalinity of the stucco material normally neutralizes during the curing process, this residue can create discoloration. The presence of alkali may also cause expansion and subsequent cracks.

A synthetic stucco system called EIFS (exterior insulation and finish system) is also widely used for residential applications, typically over studs and wood sheathing. The material can suffer from water problems unless applied correctly. If you are looking into EIFS, bear in mind that newer products make provisions for carrying off water and condensation—for example, by using an insulating base with drainage grooves.

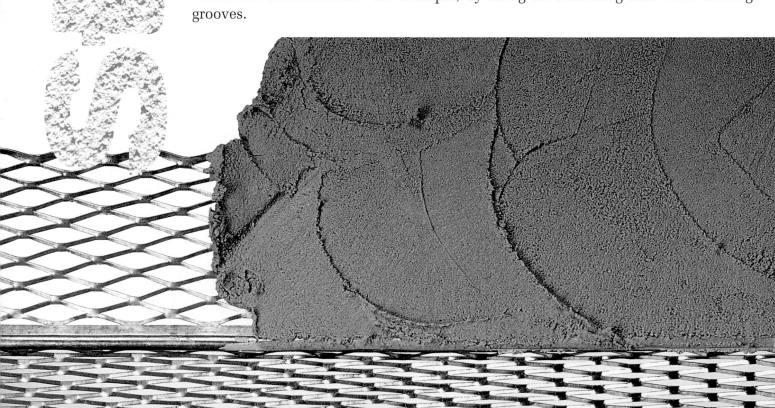

Stucco Mixes

The easiest way to make stucco is with a commercially prepared dry mix. The mix usually comes in 60-pound bags; all you need to do is add water. You can mix the stucco in a wheelbarrow using a hoe or shovel. On large siding projects, mixing is much easier if you rent a plaster-mortar mixer. A good stucco mix is easy to spread and trowel, sticking to the base to which it's applied.

To proportion your own stucco mix, add three to five parts mortar sand to one part portland cement. (The exact proportions depend on the grade of the sand.) To make home-proportioned stucco more workable, you can add Type S hydrated lime—up to 25 percent by volume of the cement. Masonry cement may be substituted for portland cement, with the same proportions. In this case, hydrated lime is not added because these cements already contain plasticizers.

To apply stucco, you can use the same tools you use with concrete work. The only additional tool you'll need is a pair of tin snips to cut wire mesh. You also might need a rubber float if you want to create a sand texture finish.

Stucco Beads and Moldings

Moldings are used at the bottom, sides, and top of stucco panels. They not only help you to gauge the ⅞-inch thickness, used at the bottom, but allow any wayward water entering the wall through cracks to escape and drip clear of the structure. What's more, metal bases and moldings separate dissimilar materials on the structure. This allows the stucco to expand and contract independent of the structure, and reduces cracking.

Moldings include screeds, beads, corners, and control joints. Casing beads provide a finished edge around the perimeter of a stucco panel. Screeds establish the thickness of the stucco. Typically, the molding has a solid edge attached to a flange of reinforcing mesh that is nailed or screwed to the structure.

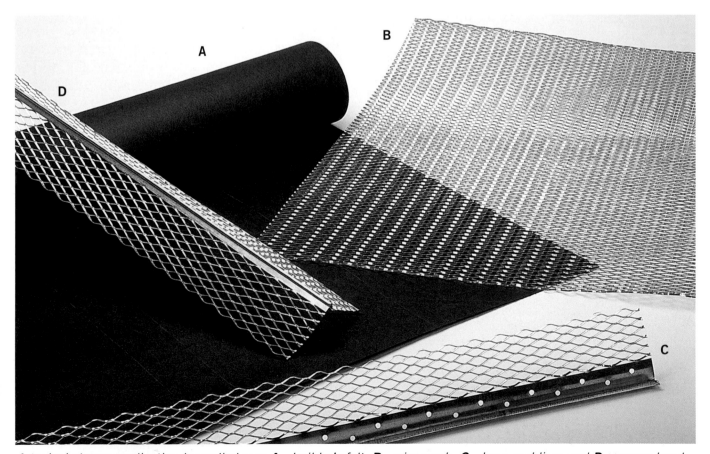

*A typical stucco application is applied over **A**—builder's felt, **B**—wire mesh, **C**—base molding, and **D**—corner bead.*

CHAPTER 5 Stucco

You can mold stucco to create deepset openings.

Fiber-Reinforced Stucco

A fiber-reinforced cement—usually containing glass fibers—adds strength, waterproofing, and durability. Fiber-reinforced cements and mortars are mixed with water and allowed to slack for a couple of minutes before a final mixing, following instructions on the package. Troweled over the face of a dry-laid concrete block or brick wall to a depth of ⅛ inch to ¼ inch, the coating takes the place of mortar bedding. The surface can be troweled smooth or textured, used as a final coat or as a base coat for other stucco. The cement is available in 50-pound bags, covering about 1 square foot per pound to a ⅛-inch depth. If an admixture similar to concrete bonder is used, the single-layer coating need not be cured. Otherwise, it should be cured with a fine mist from a garden hose two or three times a day for several days.

Setting Up the Job

When you have the materials and tools on hand, it's wise to choose an overcast day to stucco walls with a southern exposure. Excessive heat can dry the stucco prematurely, which causes shrinking and cracking. Conversely, cool temperatures make the stucco too stiff for proper troweling. Ideal temperatures for installing stucco range between 50° and 80° F. As always, it pays to mix the amount you can reasonably apply before the stucco starts to set up.

Mixing Stucco

BASE AND FINISH COAT PROPORTIONS

Base Coat and Brown Coat
   3 parts sand
   2 parts portland cement
   1 part masonry cement
   Water

Finish Coat
   1 part lime
   3 parts sand
   6 parts white cement (tint optional)
   Water

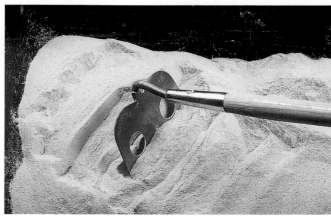

1 ***Combine the dry ingredients*** *in a clean wheelbarrow or mixing tub using a hoe with holes.*

ADDING COLORANT

A typical stucco mix with the right amount of water produces a light gray or off-white material. Of course, you could add color by painting the cured surface. But to avoid the ongoing maintenance of scraping and repainting you can color the stucco itself. Add colorant to small test batches and let them dry. Write down the proportions so when you get the right match you can re-recreate the color.

STANDARD MIX COLOR

PARTIAL TINT

MAXIMUM TINT

2 *Add water* according to manufacturer's instructions. You'll need extra water for finish coats.

3 *A properly proportioned mix* should be smooth but hold sharp edges made with a trowel.

Stucco Finishes

You can use a trowel, float, or almost any tool to create a particular surface pattern. But you should choose a design that is easy to re-create in a repeating pattern across a large wall. Experiment with some basic finishes, such as swirls made with a trowel or stipples made with a brush or damp sponge.

One popular surface treatment for stucco is a textured sand finish. After the top coat of stucco is firm, work the entire surface with a sponge float. Move the float in overlapping arcs to bring sand particles to the surface. If the float digs at any point, give the stucco more time to harden and repeat the procedure.

Adding Color

You can add color to the finish coat by mixing in colorant. Before making a final decision, test several small batches with different amounts of colorant, finish each sample as you intend to finish the wall, and let it dry.

Painting Stucco

A good paint job should last on stucco as long as it will on other exterior surfaces. But fresh masonry contains alkaline materials that can burn through fresh paint the way salt eats through an ice-covered sidewalk. The alkalinity normally neutralizes by reacting with carbon dioxide in the air, but the complete curing process may take a year.

Before painting, clear away any surface flaking or deposits of efflouresence with a stiff brush. Then wash off the remaining residue with a 3- to 5-percent solution of muriatic acid, closely following the manufacturer's cautions. Finally, rinse the wall with water.

Over new walls that have cured for less than 30 days, use an alkali-resistant primer and a 100-percent acrylic latex exterior top coat. On stucco that has cured at least a month, use a 100-percent acrylic exterior paint without a primer. Never paint less than 24 hours after rain or when rain is expected within 24 hours.

DRAINABLE EIFS APPLICATIONS

Board Drainage

Mat Drainage

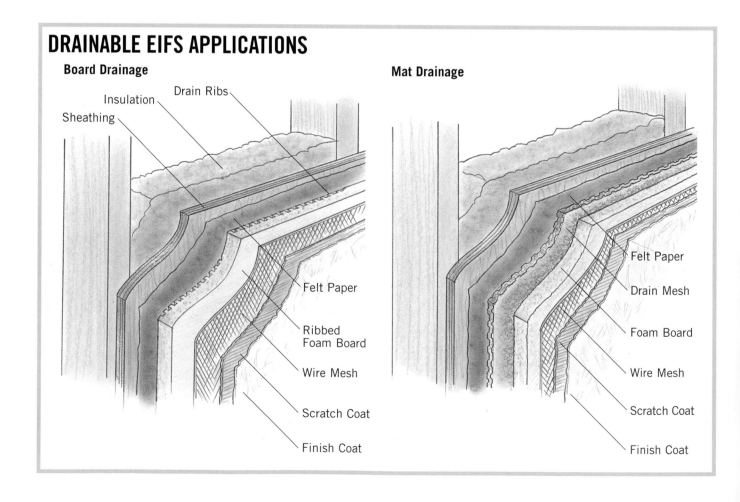

Evaluating EIFS Stucco

Exterior Insulation and Finish System (EIFS) material, also called synthetic stucco, is available in two basic configurations, both of which resemble traditional stucco. Barrier EIFS consists of foam board fixed directly over wall sheathing to which a two-layered finish coat is applied. Drainable EIFS uses either ribbed foam board or a special drainage mat to release water and moisture that can be trapped in the wall.

The foam board adds significant insulating value to the wall, limiting heat loss through the framing bays and the framing itself. The synthetic finish is aesthetically attractive to many people due to the variety of colors and textures available and the architectural features that can be created, such as corner blocks and moldings.

EIFS is among the more expensive finishes available. Installed costs for these systems often are more than twice as much as for vinyl siding. Typically, drainable EIFS costs 15 to 20 percent more than barrier EIFS systems.

Many houses with standard EIFS barrier systems have had problems with rot caused by water trapped in the EIFS covering. Problems may arise from poor installation, inadequate flashing at seams, or movement between building components. Whatever the cause, trapped water can gradually rot sheathing and framing.

Although many EIFS houses have barrier systems that work well, some mortgage lenders and insurers will not finance or insure houses with EIFS due to the reported problems. Also, some building codes now restrict the use of EIFS, while others require third-party installation inspections.

Drainable EIFS configurations were developed to prevent these problems. One of the most common uses foam board with closely set grooves on the back. The grooves run from the base molding up the entire wall and are designed to release any trapped water. Another configuration uses a drainage mat under the foam. It consists of a porous mesh through which water can drain.

Synthetic stucco, or EIFS, allows installers to create moldings and other architectural details in the surface.

CHAPTER 5 Stucco

Applications

You can apply stucco over a block or concrete wall, such as a foundation wall below siding, and over sheathing on a framed wall. Because masonry is more rigid than wood framing, you don't need as many reinforcing layers over block as you do over sheathing.

Stucco over Plywood

Applied over plywood, stucco is reinforced with steel mesh backed by two layers (or overlapped layers) of building felt paper. The stucco itself is applied in two or three layers. The first layer is called the scratch coat. It is about ⅜ inch thick, and designed to embed the reinforcement in stucco. The scratch coat gets textured to help hold the second layer tightly to it. The second layer is called the brown coat. It too is about ⅜ inch thick. Not brown at all, the brown coat serves two purposes: to provide a uniformly fin-

ished plane and to provide uniform plaster suction over the entire surface. Typically, a ⅛-inch-thick third layer of stucco, called the finish or color coat, can be applied over it instead of painting. The color coat presents both a colored and textured finished surface. If a color coat is not used, the scratch coat and brown coat are applied thicker to create the nearly 1-inch overall thickness.

Because a stronger, stiffer frame is less likely to shift and cause cracks in stucco, consider using 2x6 instead of standard 2x4 framing.

Stucco over Block

Stucco provides a good finish for concrete and block because it's made with portland cement and bonds without reinforcement. Stucco hides mortar joints in blocks and it helps to weatherproof the wall. If you are building a block wall to be covered with stucco, don't tool the joints. Strike them flush with the blocks instead.

For a typical garden wall, you won't need any

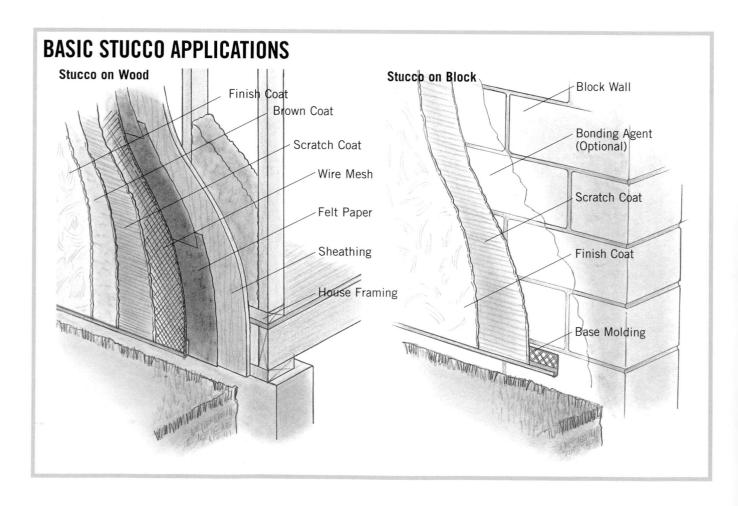

BASIC STUCCO APPLICATIONS

Stucco on Wood

Finish Coat
Brown Coat
Scratch Coat
Wire Mesh
Felt Paper
Sheathing
House Framing

Stucco on Block

Block Wall
Bonding Agent (Optional)
Scratch Coat
Finish Coat
Base Molding

Installing Stucco

TOOLS
- Hammer
- Trowel
- Raking tool

MATERIALS
- Base molding and nails
- Wire mesh
- Stucco

1 *Attach the base strip* to the bottom of the wall, following a level line snapped with a chalk line.

2 *Use galvanized nails* to fasten wire lath over the entire surface, lapping base and corner beads.

3 *Trowel out* the base coat using enough pressure to embed the mix into the wire lath.

4 *Scratch the surface* of the base coat with horizontal grooves to create a bond between coats.

5 *Trowel on a brown coat* that is ⅜ in. thick. Paint the surface or add a finish coat that is ⅛ in. thick.

CHAPTER 5

Stucco

stucco edge moldings except on long walls where you place the moldings over the control joints in the block.

To create a good bond for stucco, the surface of the concrete block must be clean and free of dust, efflorescence, grease, and paint. A new block wall should present no problems, but older walls need to be checked for suction. Good suction makes for a good bond. To check suction, spray water on the surface and watch to see whether the water is absorbed—sucked in—by the surface. If it is, the wall has suction. But if the water beads up in droplets, as on a window pane, the suction is poor. On the other hand, suction is too great if the surface absorbs water immediately. This condition can be controlled by spraying (not soaking) the wall several times just before stuccoing. If a good bond is doubtful, apply a concrete bonding agent to the wall.

No matter what the backing or finish, stucco should be moist-cured for 48 hours to attain maximum strength and durability.

In most climates, moist curing can be accomplished by spraying the stucco at the beginning and end of each day with a fine mist from a garden hose. In dry climates or hot weather you should spray more often. You can drape plastic sheeting to protect fresh stucco from rain.

Stucco is appropriate for a variety of different home styles, from traditional to contemporary.

SURFACE TEXTURES

FLOATED SMOOTH

SPONGE SWIRLED

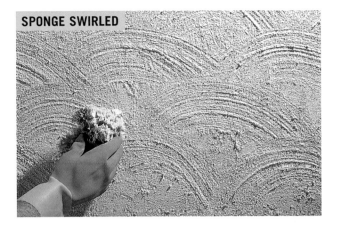

BRUSH LINED

BRUSH SPLATTERED

FLATTENED SPLATTER

BOARD DRAGGED

TROWEL SWIRLED

TROWEL RIDGED

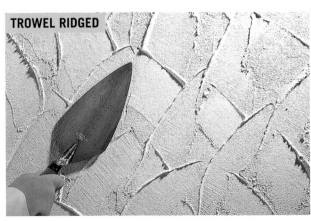

CHAPTER 5 **Stucco**

Maintenance and Repair

You can clean sound stucco with a garden hose and spray head, or use a pressure washer. But before you hit the stucco with pressurized water, wash it down gently with clean water from bottom to top. This keeps any soil washed from upper portions of the wall from soaking into lower portions. Avoid blasting the surface directly with high pressure. Instead, hit the wall with a glancing stream from a fan nozzle.

Make it a point to fix cracks in stucco as soon as you detect them. Even small cracks will let water seep into the underlying structure, where it will eventually cause damage. Over time, water and the winter freeze-thaw cycles will turn minor cracks into major problems.

Clear out large cracks and gaps, and patch them with the same stucco mix that was used on the walls. Fill small cracks with all-acrylic or siliconized-acrylic sealants.

Stucco can be difficult to color-match. If the surface requires many patches, it may be easier to cover it with a cement-based paint or an acrylic exterior paint. But let the stucco patches cure for at least 30 days, and dampen the wall with water before painting.

Repairing a Stucco Wall

TOOLS

- Work gloves
- Safety glasses
- Metal shears
- Hammer and cold chisel
- Whisk broom (or texturing tool)
- Trowel
- Pry bar

MATERIALS

- Stucco or patch compound
- Wire mesh
- Galvanized nails or screws

1 *Break away loose material* with a hammer and masonry chisel. Wear gloves and safety glasses.

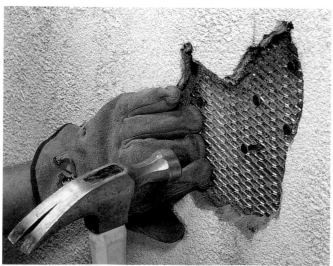

4 *Fasten the mesh* using galvanized nails or screws. Apply concrete bonder to the edges of the hole.

5 *Trowel a scratch coat* of stucco into the dampened patch area using a mason's trowel.

CAULKING CRACKS

E ven small cracks can be fatal flaws in a stucco wall. That's because they let in water that causes a variety of problems, including rotting the supporting structure. Cracks are most common around windows and doors. You should clean them out with a brush or compressed air and seal them with a flexible, exterior-grade caulk, such as silicone.

2 *Lift loose and broken stucco* out of the wall with a pry bar or the end of the screwdriver.

3 *Cut a patch of metal mesh* about the size and shape of the hole using metal shears.

6 *Use the tip of a trowel* to give the scratch coat some tooth, creating shallow horizontal grooves.

7 *Apply the finish coat,* and texture it to blend in with the surrounding stucco wall.

Repairing Damaged Stucco

It's easy to repair holes, crumbling, and chipped corners in stucco. Start by scraping out any loose, crumbly stucco, and snipping out any damaged or corroded mesh. Then dampen the area with water.

You need to reinforce the hole only if you are repairing stucco on plywood. If the hole is large or contains no reinforcement, use metal shears to cut a piece of metal mesh (also called wire lath) to fit the opening. Fasten the lath with 1-inch galvanized deck screws. Apply concrete bonder to the edges of the patch using a brush or roller. If the repair is over brick or block, apply bonder to the bottom of the hole as well.

Wait for the bonder to become tacky. Then mix standard stucco using less water to make it thicker, or purchase a stucco patching compound with texturizer. Trowel on the mix in a layer about ¼ inch thick. Let this layer set until firm. Build up layers until the patch is about ⅛ inch below the surface. Then scratch the patch with a piece of hardware cloth or wire mesh.

Mix finish-coat stucco to match the existing color, and apply a thin coat to level the patch with the wall. Texture the patch with a trowel, float, or sponge to make it blend with the texture of the surrounding area.

Finally, cure the patch by taping plastic over the area. Wait at least two days before removing the plastic.

USING A HOPPER-SPRAYER

Over large areas, consider renting a hopper-sprayer. This compressor-driven (air-powered) tool allows you to apply a large amount of material without reloading. Or you can create surface textures with a brush and trowel, basically splattering a smooth layer of stucco with a secondary partial coat.

Using a stucco sprayer *can speed up the work.*

Stucco can be finished with clean, sharp edges or molded into rounded-over corners.

Repairing a Stucco Corner

TOOLS
- Hammer and cold chisel
- Hacksaw
- Trowel
- Float

MATERIALS
- Mesh corner bead
- Galvanized nails or screws
- Stucco

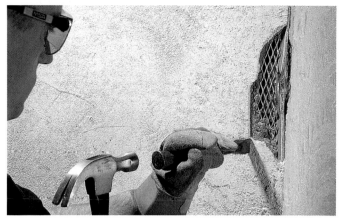

1 *Chip out enough of the stucco* to expose the edges of the damaged mesh corner bead.

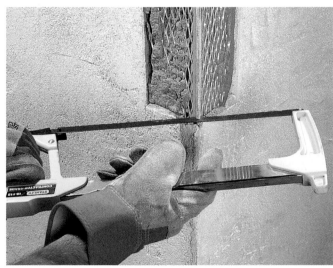

2 *Cut out* the damaged portion of the metal corner bead using a hacksaw.

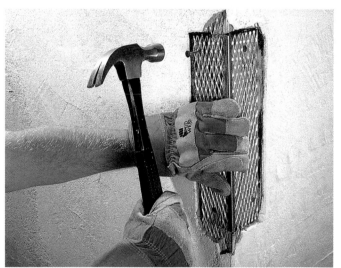

3 *Nail a new section of corner bead* onto the corner of the building.

4 *Apply a scratch coat* to the corner bead. Scratch lines into it with the tip of a trowel.

5 *Trowel a finish coat* over the scratch coat after it has dried. Texture the finish coat to match.

CHAPTER 5 Stucco

Stucco is a traditional finish for block walls and for the exposed portion of a house foundation. It's easier to apply over solid masonry than over wood framing for several reasons. First, block is rigid, so you don't need to add reinforcing mesh. (But you should add base and corner beads.) Also, masonry generally needs only two coats: a base, or scratch, coat about ⅜ in. thick, and a finish coat about ¼ in.

thick. Without reinforcing mesh, you should prepare older walls by patching cracks, breaking off protruding mortar in joints, and scraping or wire brushing surface deposits. For good adhesion you need a clean wall. Improve the bond by rolling on a layer of masonry bonding agent. Mix stucco with water for at least three minutes. One 60-lb. bag is about all you can apply before the mix starts to set.

Stucco on Block

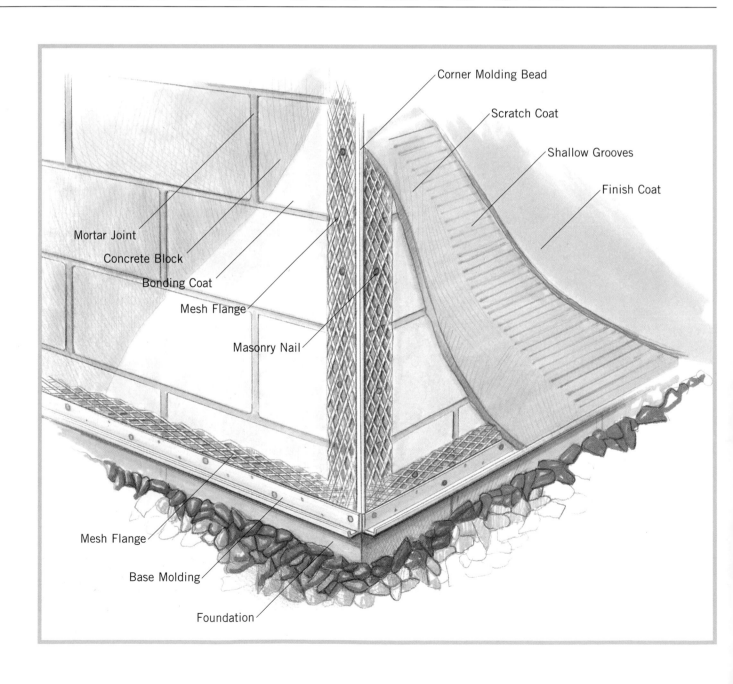

Stucco on Block Installation

TOOLS

- Work gloves
- Cold chisel and hammer
- Wire brush
- Roller
- Mixing tray
- Spray bottle or water hose
- Level
- Trowels
- Raking tool
- Finishing float

MATERIALS

- Masonry bonding agent
- Base and corner bead
- Masonry nails
- Stucco mix
- Plastic sheeting

SMART JOB TIP

Stucco has to moist-cure for at least 48 hours in order to achieve maximum hardness. You can spray the surface regularly to keep it damp, but it's more practical to lock in the moisture with plastic sheeting. If you plan to paint (or add a thin color coat), let the surface dry for two days after the 48-hour curing period.

CHAPTER 5   Stucco

1 *Use a cold chisel* and heavy hammer to remove any excess mortar from the block joints.

2 *Scrape off dirt* and other deposits, such as efflorescence, with a wire brush.

3 *Roll on a masonry bonding agent* to improve adhesion over old walls, not necessary on new block.

4 *Install a base drip bead* to stop the stucco finish and trim the edge just short of the ground.

MAKING A RAKING TOOL

There are many ways to make a raking tool that allows you to scratch horizontal grooves into the scratch coat. This one is simply a piece of 1x2 with galvanized roofing nails driven through on ¾-in. centers. In another stucco project (page 149, Step 8) the same effect is achieved with a piece of paint strainer with its edge bent over and alternate strips cut off.

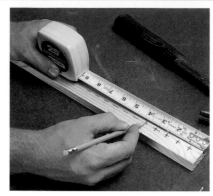

Mark and predrill holes on ¾-in. centers down the middle of a 1x2.

A row of galvanized nail points will make a uniform series of rakes.

5 **Use a corner bead** with mesh flanges to make the transition around block corners.

6 **Use a mixing tray** to make just enough workable mix to spread on the wall at one time.

9 **After the scratch coat has set up**, spray it down with water to help the final coat adhere.

10 **Spread out the finish coat** with a trowel, smoothing it in a layer about ¼ in. thick.

FINISHING OPTIONS

There are many ways to finish stucco. You can smooth out the top coat, create a more textured appearance using a float with a rubber face (right), or use the edge of a metal trowel to make shallow indentations (far right). Generally, a distinct pattern, such as a swirl shape, looks best if each element is about the same size and applied with even spacing.

A rubber float will leave a slightly rough and sandy looking surface.

A finish float can be used to make a variety of patterns.

7 *Use a trowel* in upward strokes to apply the first coat. You can also use a hawk to hold more mix.

8 *Before the first coat sets up,* scratch in grooves. This raking tool is homemade but effective.

11 *Clean excess stucco off the corners* by running a trowel along the edge of the metal bead.

12 *Cover the wall with plastic* to seal in moisture for 48 hours and allow the stucco to cure.

CHAPTER 5 **Stucco**

When you apply stucco over a wood-frame wall, there is always the risk that settling or even minor seasonal movement in the frame will crack the rigid stucco surface. There are two ways to guard against damage. One is to build a rigid wall—for example, with 2x6s instead of 2x4s or at least to add let-in bracing as a stiffener. The other is to apply reinforcing mesh (plus corner and base beads with mesh flanges) to the wall surface. You also need to protect the sheathing with overlapped felt paper. The stucco itself is built up in three layers over frame walls. Start with a scratch coat about ⅜ inch thick, scored to help the second layer adhere. The next coat, called the brown coat, about ¼ inch thick, provides a uniformly smooth surface. The ⅛-inch-thick third layer, called the color coat, can be tinted and textured to suit.

Stucco on Wood

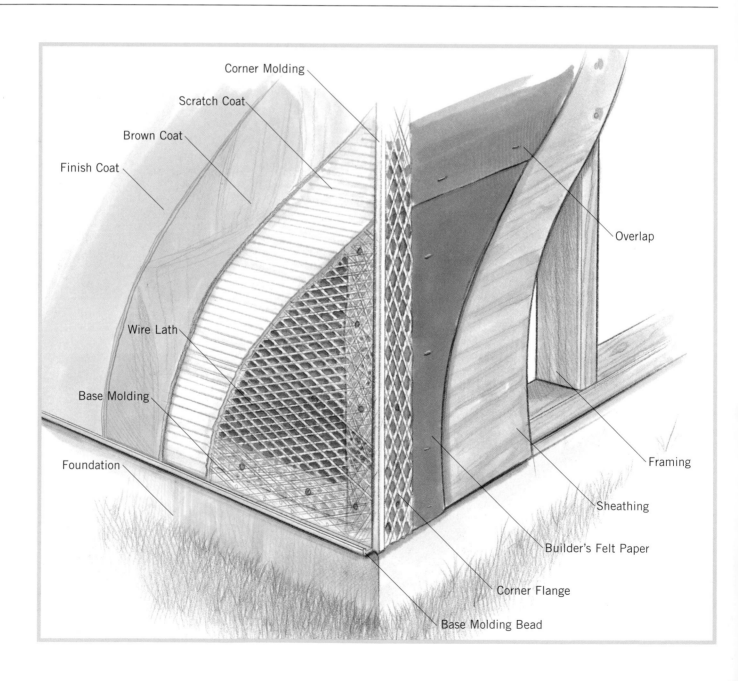

Stucco on Wood Installation

TOOLS
- Work gloves
- Hammer and stapler
- Utility knife and aviation shears
- Chalk-line box
- Cement mixer or wheelbarrow
- Raking tool
- Mortar hawk and trowels
- Shovel
- Spray bottle

MATERIALS
- Felt paper
- Self-furring metal lath
- Lath base and corner bead
- Galvanized roofing nails
- Stucco mix
- Color tint (optional)
- Staples

SMART JOB TIP
Minimize the loss of material and keep the work area clean by applying stucco using a mortar hawk for your trowel. The hawk is basically a platform you hold against the wall in one hand while you spread the mix with a trowel. As you work, excess material falls back onto the hawk so that you can reuse it.

CHAPTER 5 **Stucco**

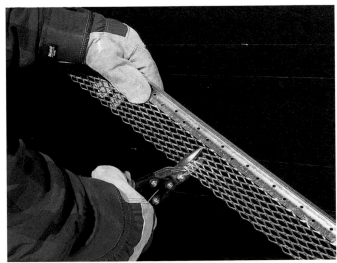
1 *Staple felt paper* to the sheathing, wrapping corners and providing a liberal overlap at courses.

2 *Snap a level chalk line* on the felt paper above the foundation as a guide for the base bead.

3 *Measure the mesh-edged base bead,* and trim it to length using aviation snips.

4 *Set the mesh flange up,* aligned with your level guideline, and secure the bead with roofing nails.

TEXTURING STUCCO

You can finish stucco by adding a top coat to the surface however you like, but experiment on a test patch first. You can trowel out a smooth finish or use the trowel edge to create a shallow pattern. Some floats produce a slightly rougher surface. You can use them to make swirls and other patterns. A dash surface (right) creates a deeper texture employing an extra layer of stucco.

To create a wet-dash finish, snap on mix with a whisk broom.

To create a trowel-dash finish, flatten out blobs with a trowel.

5 **Install metal lath** with galvanized roofing nails or staples to form a continuous layer of support.

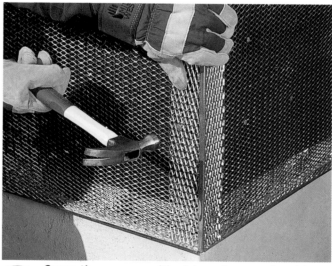

6 **Cover the corners** with strips of corner bead to make a neat edge between wall surfaces.

9 **Moisten the surface** of the scratch coat before applying the second layer, called the brown coat.

10 **Use a long trowel or float** to spread out the brown coat in an even layer.

MIXING STUCCO

To apply a uniform finish you need a consistent mix. Following mix directions on the bag, you should get a plastic mix that doesn't run. If you add colorant to the final smoothing coat, add a little more water to establish uniform proportions so that you can re-create the same tint even when mixing small batches to spread before the stucco sets up.

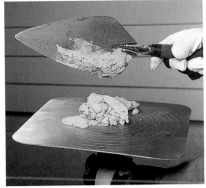

A good mix should hold to the hawk and trowel without running.

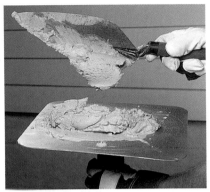

A bad mix with too much water will slip off a trowel and puddle.

7 **Work with an upward motion** of your trowel to fully embed the first course into the lath.

8 **Scratch horizontal lines** into the surface, using this homemade tool, a piece of paint-straining screen.

11 **You can add powdered colorant** to the stucco mix to tint the final coat, if desired.

12 **Smooth out the last coat,** keeping this final layer about ⅛ in. thick.

Stucco
Gallery

Stucco is basically a hard masonry shell that you can apply in a wide variety of patterns to dress up both solid masonry and wood-framed surfaces. It lets you create rounded corners and uniquely layered applications that are durable and weather resistant on inside and outside walls.

Using a variety of elements adds to a design. Stone, stucco, and concrete create an appealing fountain and walkway (opposite).

Although it's often praised for its ability to form curves, stucco is also a good choice in "edgier" designs (right).

Trowel wet stucco to create a wide variety of patterns. Stucco creates a scalloped backdrop (below left).

Authentic Southwestern style (below right) is only attainable with stucco. Other materials can't match its contours.

CHAPTER 5 Stucco

Apply stucco in rough, hard-worked layers for an interesting effect (opposite top left).

Use stucco inside or out. This courtyard (opposite top right) is enhanced with rough stucco walls.

Smooth out stucco to form distinctive curved edges (opposite bottom left).

Custom designs are easy with stucco. A mantel (opposite bottom right) is created from smooth stucco.

Stucco offers the opportunity to create a variety of surface finishes, from smooth to roughly pebbled (below).

CHAPTER 5 Stucco

Brick

Materials
Patterns
Reinforcing
Mortar
Setting
Maintenance and Repair
Projects

CHAPTER **6**

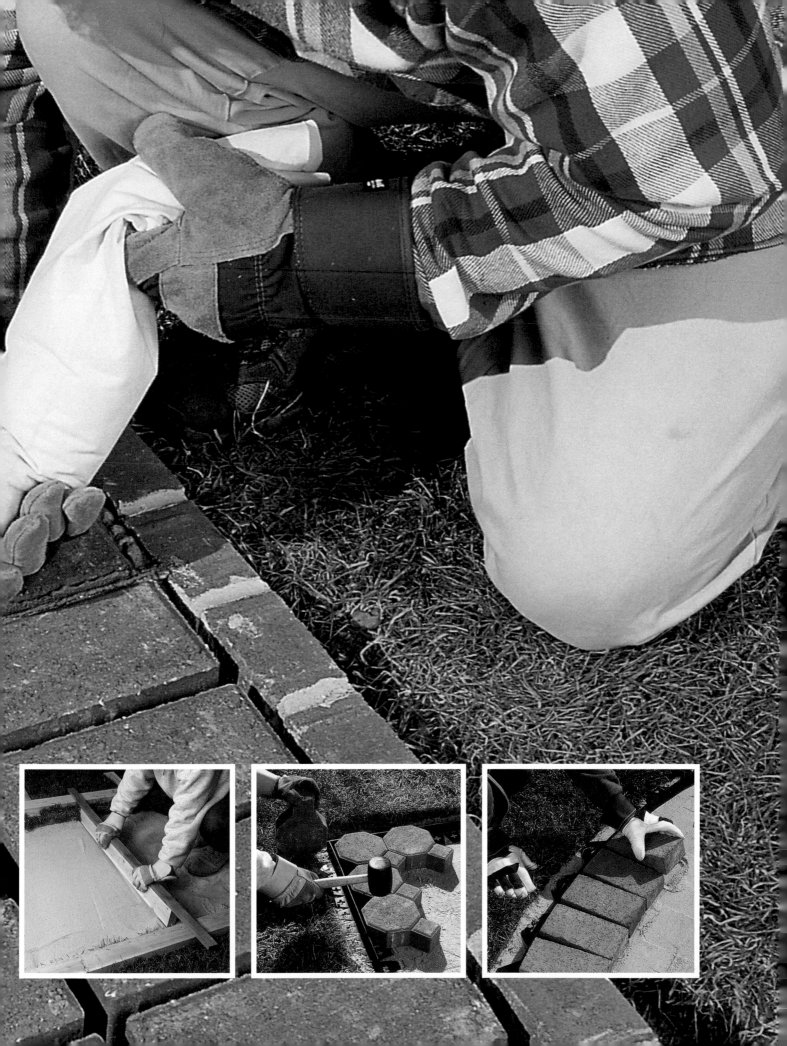

Materials

In one form or another, brick has been used as a building material for thousands of years. It is durable, attractive, and noncombustible, among other things, and installing it is a straightforward job. The work is well suited to do-it-yourselfers because you can do it a little at a time.

Bricks are bonded together with mortar. But most projects will also require accessories such as anchors, ties, or joint reinforcements. These materials can strengthen the overall structure, will anchor masonry to existing construction, and will control expansion and contraction.

Types of Brick

Brick is made from molded clay that is fired at very high temperatures in a kiln. The clay color and firing temperature determine the brick color, although some manufacturers combine clays to produce tones from off-white to almost black. Brick textures vary too, depending on the molding process.

Brick made in the United States and Canada today is extremely dense, hard, and durable. If the bricks are shaped by extruding clay through a die, they usually have large holes through the middle. The holes make the bricks lighter and improve the mortar bond. This type of brick is most commonly used for wall construction, where the holes are not visible.

To choose brick for your project, visit a local supplier and look at sample panels. Bear in mind that bricks with a wide range of light and dark shades can be more difficult to work with than bricks of a single color.

Face Brick. A batch of face brick will be quite uniform in color, size, and texture. It comes in three types. Type FBA (architectural) brick has no limits on size variations or on the amount of chips and cracks that are permitted. This type is popular for residential work because the units resemble old brick. Type FBS (standard) and FBX (extra) have tighter limits on variations and are generally used on commercial jobs.

Bricks similar to those used in historic buildings are still produced by some manufacturers. But they will absorb

Common Brick Types

Face Bricks *are uniform in color and texture.*

Modular Building Bricks *are often rough-faced.*

Locking Pavers *nestle together without mortar.*

Firebrick *is baked at high temperature to resist heat.*

Brick Pavers *are strong and weatherproof.*

Veneer Bricks *are thin slices of real brick.*

CHAPTER 6 **Brick**

more water than extruded bricks. You could also work with genuine used brick, but unpredictable durability makes them risky for exterior use.

Modular Building Brick. Building bricks, or common bricks, are rougher in appearance and less expensive than face bricks, but are structurally sound. Most building bricks today are sold with interior holes that reduce weight.

Paving Brick. Paving brick is manufactured to be denser than the other bricks because in paving, the widest faces are visible. The clay is machine-pressed densely into molds and baked longer than either extruded or molded face bricks. This process reduces the amount of water that will be absorbed by the brick.

With pavers, low absorption is critical because the materials must be able to withstand repeated cycles of winter freezing and thawing as well as heavy traffic. Paving brick is classified by its appearance in the same way as face brick: PA (architectural), PS (standard), and PX (extra).

Firebrick. Firebrick is made of a special clay that is baked at an extremely high temperature. It is used to line fireplaces and is generally a yellowish off-white color. You must install it with a special fireclay mortar.

WATER TESTING AND GRADING

Very dry brick absorbs much of the water in fresh mortar, weakening the bond. To test for excessive absorption, place 12 drops of water on any spot on the brick. If the water is absorbed in less than one minute, the brick is too dry, and you should wet the bricks as you install them. Overall grading is based on resistance to freeze-thaw damage. Grade MW (moderate weathering) can be exposed to moisture but not freezing. Grade SW (severe weathering) is used when the bricks are likely to be frozen when saturated. Grade NW (no weathering) is for indoor use only.

Using a Brick Splitter

1 **Measure your brick** and mark the length required to fill the void, allowing for mortar joints.

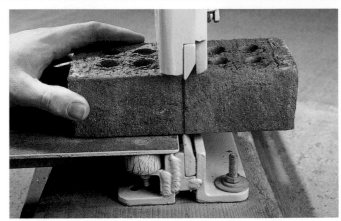

2 **Line up your squared mark** with the angled cutting blades in the jaws of the brick splitter.

LAYOUTS AND ESTIMATES

L aying out bricks is simple when you set them to a multiple of 4 inches. This multiple also applies against 8 x 8 x 16-inch concrete block. With 8-inch brick, the 4-inch module is the length of half bricks that create a staggered layout. For example, make a brick wall a multiple of 4 inches long (80 inches long rather than 78 inches). For estimating purposes, figure about seven bricks (nominally 4 x 8 inches) for every square foot of area in a wall. Estimate about 4½ bricks for every square foot when laying paving bricks broad faced, horizontally on the ground.

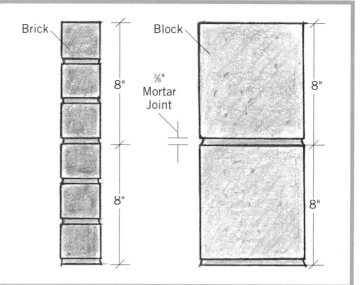

COMMON BRICK SIZES

T he basic modular unit is 3⅝ inches wide, 2¼ inches thick, and 7⅝ inches long. When laid with standard ⅜-inch mortar joints, the nominal length becomes about 8 inches. Three bricks laid on top of one another with ⅜-inch mortar joints measure 8 inches high. Paving bricks designed to butt together without mortar have a full 4 x 8-inch face. The most common are 1 inch thick for light traffic areas and 2¼ inches for heavy traffic areas, such as driveways and streets. Some suppliers offer special shapes such as copings and angled corner bricks that fit a modular system.

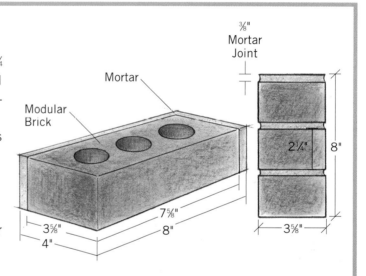

3 **Push down** slowly on the lever, compressing the upper and lower jaws until the brick snaps.

4 **The blades** of a brick splitter produce a cleaner cut than you can make with hammer and chisel.

Brick Patterns

Bricks and pavers come in so many sizes and shapes that you can create an almost endless number of patterns.

The most common bond pattern is called a running bond. In a wall with this pattern bricks are laid flat on their wide surface and run lengthwise. Each brick in a course of stretchers is offset by one-half brick from the bricks in the courses above and below.

This bond is also generally used on walks, which don't present the same structural consid-erations as walls do. And staggered joints tend to hold together better than joints that are aligned in a row. There are variations, such as using an offset of one-third or one-quarter brick in each course. But a running bond works well in any landscape and is easy to keep consistent, whether you are using bricks set with mortar joints or pavers butted without mortar.

Bear in mind that any layout becomes more complicated when you introduce curves, more common in walks than in walls. You can make some adjustments in the joints to run the brick in line with the walk or set the running bond so that the bricks are all parallel with each other.

This mortared running bond curves with the walk.

This curved walk has a rigid, parallel running bond.

PAVER PATTERNS

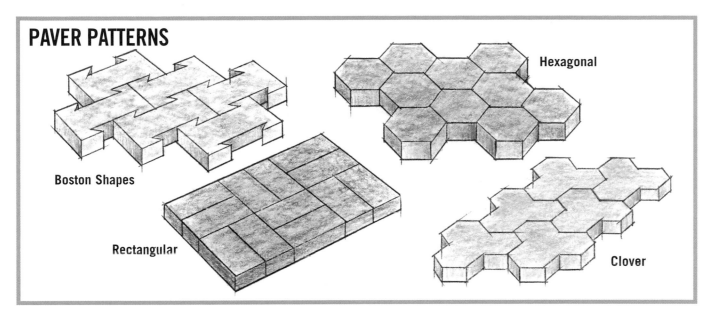

Boston Shapes

Rectangular

Hexagonal

Clover

This informal garden walk has an organic pattern.

A herringbone pattern is more complex to lay out.

When you need to turn a corner in a wall, bricks called headers are turned perpendicular to the stretcher courses. Also by alternating header and stretcher bricks in different ways, you can create a variety of patterns. And because header units help hold the two wythes, or brick widths, of a wall together, they are functional as well as decorative. A number of decorative bond patterns mimic the look of historic masonry buildings.

Other popular bond patterns include the common, or American, bond. It is similar to the running bond, except that it has courses of headers spaced every sixth course. The English bond consists of alternating courses of stretchers and headers; the headers are centered over the stretchers, and the vertical joints of all the stretcher courses align.

A stack bond lays all the bricks as either headers or stretchers with all joints aligning vertically. But the stack bond is weak structurally, and generally not permitted for load-bearing walls without reinforcement in the joints.

The Flemish bond is a complex pattern in which every course has alternating stretchers and headers. The pattern is offset by courses so that the headers center over stretchers and vice versa. Remember that more complex patterns often require more cutting.

Brick lends itself well to traditional home exteriors like this one.

BRICK PATTERNS

RUNNING

ENGLISH

COMMON

DUTCH

GARDEN WALL

FLEMISH

Reinforcing Brick

Although brick is very strong in compression (stacked on top of each other), there are many situations where it needs a variety of mechanical helpers to resist lateral forces and toppling. For example, multiple wythes of masonry in a wall must be tied together either with header bricks or metal ties.

You can use S-shaped wire reinforcers to tie wythes together whether they are built face to face with a mortar joint between them or separated by an airspace. You can also use corrugated strap-type ties in this situation. Corrugated ties can also be used to tie brick and concrete block together.

One of the most common installations that needs reinforcement is a brick veneer wall. The wall looks as though it is load bearing but isn't. The wall is actually set away from the house structure to create an airspace and allow airflow to prevent condensation.

You need to reinforce and provide lateral support for the brick veneer by attaching it to the house wall with corrugated veneer anchors. Generally, you should connect anchors to wood framing or concrete every 16 inches vertically and every 32 inches horizontally. For adequate strength, be sure that you nail the anchors through the sheathing into the studs.

Masonry ties, anchors, and joint reinforcement should always be placed in the mortar rather than directly on the brick. This means that you start with a standard application of mortar in the joint, press the tie into place, and then add more mortar on top of the tie to fill. For extra protection against corrosion, use ties that are hot-dip galvanized.

Strengthening Mortar Joints

Metal reinforcement can make a wall stronger and tie together double-wythe walls. But it is no substitute for fully-filled mortar joints that transfer loads down the wall, brick to brick. When the mortar fails, loads will concentrate instead of spreading evenly, and walls can crack apart.

The first signs of trouble are often hairline cracks in the joints. They can let moisture seep into the wall and gradually wash away more mortar. During the winter, water can freeze and exert more pressure on the mortar. In a typical cycle of deterioration, small cracks widen, letting in more water, which causes more erosion. This, in turn, widens the cracks until chunks of mortar fall out and leave bricks unsupported.

To solidify walls with cracked joints, scrape out old material. The rule of thumb is to excavate old joints at least as deep as they are wide (up to twice as wide). Then brush out the joints, and dampen them. With fresh mortar on a trowel or hawk, push mortar directly into the joint.

REINFORCING BRICK

You can strengthen brick walls by adding either corrugated or Z-shaped ties. When using modular bricks with interior holes, you can also insert rebar into the holes to reinforce against tipover. Rebar also can be useful to secure a brick wall to its footing. In this case, you need to space the rebar to fit the brick and insert it in the footing before the concrete hardens.

Corrugated ties *can span the gap between two wythes.*

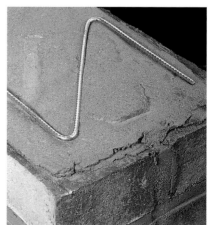
S-shaped ties *also can reinforce the joints between double walls.*

This high garden wall, with running-bond brick pattern, provides privacy for a backyard garden.

INSTALLING TIES

A brick veneer wall is built about 1 inch out from the house sheathing on either existing footings or steel angles bolted to the foundation. Secure it to the wall with metal ties. Nail the high ends into the framing at every other stud, or 32 inches horizontally. Space them about every 16 inches vertically. Fold the lower ends into the mortar between courses.

Nail ties to house framing so that the ends will float in the mortar.

Embed metal ties in the middle of the mortar between courses.

Brick Mortar

Brick mortars are mixtures of portland cement, lime, sand, and water. You can mix your own or purchase factory-blended dry mortars, which you then combine with sand and water.

Although the mortar in a masonry structure constitutes only a small percentage of the material, it is of critical importance. A good bond between the mortar and either bricks or blocks provides stability and resistance to wind and other lateral loads. It also helps prevent moisture penetration. While mortar is similar to concrete, the kinds of mixtures that produce a good bond do not necessarily produce the high compressive strengths of concrete mixes. With mortar, it's important for the mix to be workable and produce a good bond, in addition to having reasonable strength.

Mix Components. Mortar and concrete typically use the same types of portland cement. The most common is a Type I general-purpose cement. Lime is added to mortar mixes to make them retain water longer, to improve workability and handling, and to make the hardened mortar less brittle and less prone to shrinkage. The mortar in historic buildings was made with lime and

You can use combinations of bond patterns and bricks set proud of the wall face to create decorative details.

sand only. These lime mortars cured very slowly. The invention of portland cement in the late 1800s changed the way masonry mortar was made and sped up construction. The trade-off is that the higher the portland cement content, the stiffer the mixture is when it is wet and the more rigid the mortar is when it is cured. This makes the mortar a little harder to work with and a little more likely to crack if the masonry is not properly constructed.

Typical Mortar Mixes. For interior work and outdoor work that is above grade, use a Type N mix. This mix is composed of 1 part portland cement, 1 part lime, and 6 parts sand. The lime should be a hydrated mason's lime, and the sand should be a well-graded masonry sand that has a range of grain sizes from fine to coarse. For below-grade construction and for paving projects, use a Type S mix. For flatwork, including patios, sidewalks, and driveways, air-entrained portland cement will improve the mortar's freeze-thaw resistance.

Mix mortar by volume proportions using a container of convenient size. Use the container to measure out each of the ingredients according to your proportions. Always use the same container for measuring ingredients so that the proportional volumes are consistent from batch to batch.

Mortar Proportions and Mixing

MORTAR PROPORTIONS BY VOLUME

Type	Portland Cement	Hydrated Lime	Mason's Sand
Portland cement & lime mortar:			
N	1	1	6
S	1	½	4½
Factory-blended masonry cement mortar:			
N	1	n/a	3
S	1	n/a	3

1 *Mix the dry ingredients* in the mortar box to be sure that they are evenly distributed throughout.

2 *Slowly add water* to the dry mix, stirring as you go until the mix reaches the proper consistency.

3 *Mortar should be wet* but not runny. Peaks should stand up on their own.

CHAPTER 6 Brick

Setting Brick

After testing your layout with a dry run, start by laying brick from the ends and then filling in toward the middle. Spread an embedding coat of mortar that is ½ to ¾ inch thick, slightly wider than a brick, and two or three bricks long. This first course is critical—you want to lay enough mortar so that when you place the bricks, the bed joint doesn't develop voids.

Lay the corner or end brick first, seating it in the mortar. Measure to make sure that the mortar bed is the right thickness and the brick is at the right height. Tap the brick lightly with the trowel handle, if necessary, to settle it.

Buttering. Next, butter the end of the next brick with mortar by holding it in one hand and swiping mortar onto it from all four directions. Seat the second brick into the mortar bed and against the first brick, making a tight joint. If mortar doesn't squeeze out, then there isn't enough mortar in the joints. After laying each brick, trowel off excess mortar from the face of the wall.

On some types of brickwork, you'll need to install reinforcing wire or corrugated metal ties. When you install ties between a veneer wall and a house wall, make sure that each tie is embed-

Laying Brick

TOOLS
- Work gloves
- Mixing tools and trough
- Trowel
- Mason blocks and string
- Striking tool

MATERIALS
- Brick
- Mortar (cement, lime, sand, water)

1 *Spread enough mortar* to create a ⅜-in. bed. Use more to set a wider bed on the first course.

4 *Butter the head end* of the next brick, shaping the mix on all four sides with your trowel.

5 *Set the buttered brick* in place, and use the heel of your trowel to tap it into alignment.

ded with mortar surrounding it on all sides. Spread the mortar first, press the ties into place, and then add a little mortar on top to cover. The ties that are used to connect two wythes of brick are S-shaped rigid wire ties. Most codes require that rigid wire ties be spaced every 16 inches vertically (every eighth course of brick) and every 32 inches horizontally. Offset every other row of ties to create a staggered pattern.

Use mason's blocks and string to guide the courses, and check with a 4-foot level to verify plumb and level. Also, hold a story pole that is marked every 8 inches up to the lead to quickly check for correct height of the courses.

Finishing Joints. The joints are ready for tooling when you can press your thumb against the mortar and leave a print impression without any mortar sticking to your thumb. The concave joint is the most common. Concave, V, and grapevine joints are the most weather-resistant because the surface of the mortar is compacted as it is tooled.

Check the mortar frequently, and tool the joints a few at a time when the surface is just the right consistency. As you tool the joints, small pieces of mortar called tailings will be squeezed out at the edges. Remove these tailings with the edge of your trowel.

2 *Turn over the trowel,* face side in, to compact and form the outer edge of the mortar bed.

3 *Make a shallow furrow* down the center of the bed to fully support bricks along their edges.

6 *As you set bricks* to the string guide, scrape off excess mortar that oozes from the joints.

7 *As the mortar sets up,* smooth and compress the mortar in a concave shape with a striking tool.

Setting Veneer Brick

In addition to many types of full-size bricks, there are thinner types, often called veneer bricks, that can be used inside and outside of the house. Although there are brick facsimiles, synthetics, and fake bricks printed on paneling, there are also thin sections of real bricks.

The main advantage is that you get the look and even the feel of actual bricks without all of the weight. That means you don't need to worry about extending a concrete footing or bolting on a steel angle iron for support. You can set thin bricks right against the wall.

In a typical exterior installation, you need to be sure that the wall is sound and covered with an overlapped layer of builder's felt (tar paper).

For a strong bond, start with a layer of wire mesh attached to the wall framing with galvanized nails. Then trowel an embedding layer of adhesive mortar onto the mesh. Simply press the veneer bricks into the mortar, following your layout lines and leaving space for joints. String a guideline, and recheck the alignment with a level every few courses.

When the adhesive sets up (generally overnight) you can fill in the joints. It pays to use a grout bag to direct grout into the joints and to avoid smearing the surface with mortar.

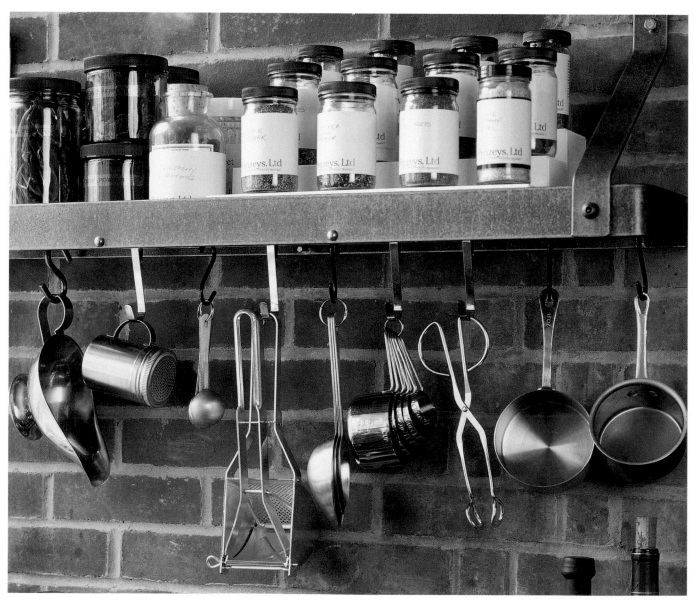

Veneer brick provides a durable and traditional wall in kitchens without wasting the space for full brick.

Laying Veneer Brick

TOOLS

- Hammer
- Hacksaw
- Trowel or float
- Striking tool

MATERIALS

- Adhesive mortar
- Veneer bricks
- Metal lath mesh
- String and line levels
- Galvanized nails or screws

1 *Use galvanized nails* to attach sheets of metal lath to the wall. This will hold the mortar to the wall.

2 *Trowel an embedding coat* of adhesive mortar onto the mesh. Work in one area at a time.

3 *Press the bricks into the mortar* leaving space for grout joints. Work to a level string line.

4 *Use a hacksaw* to cut half pieces for alternate courses so that the joints can be staggered.

5 *Smooth and compress the joints* to a uniform depth and concave shape with a striking tool.

CHAPTER 6 **Brick**

Maintenance and Repair

To evaluate a brick wall, each component must be considered. Large cracks, called faults, in the overall structure are usually the most obvious problems and the most costly to repair. Most faults can be traced to uneven settling. When soil under one section settles more than under another, the foundation and the wall above can crack under the strain.

The signs of fundamental structural problems are staircase-pattern cracking in joints along many courses of brick and either large-scale con- vex or concave cupping of the walls. You can check for this curving, which can be difficult to detect over a large surface, by using mason's blocks and string.

Evaluating Cracks. Don't write off a wall just because it has some cracks. They may be only cosmetic or the result of settling that occurred long ago. Old, stable cracks can usually be patched and sealed against the weather. They tend to look somewhat weathered and dirty and may even contain dirt, debris, or spider webs.

New, unstable cracks are usually clean, with lighter colored mortar than that on the sur- rounding wall, indicating that the building is

DIAGNOSING BRICK PROBLEMS

There are three main types of brick deteriora- tion. The most serious is staircase-pattern cracking (below), which is often a sign of major structural problems. To correct the cracking, you may first need to correct settling problems or other weaknesses in the foundation. Eroded mortar joints (right) can let water into the wall, which can cause many types of deterioration and weaken the wall. Promptly repoint eroded mortar joints. Spalling (lower right) often occurs when freezing water causes a brick to fracture—usually the face of the brick cracks off. To fix this problem you need to replace the fractured brick.

ERODED MORTAR JOINTS

STAIRCASE CRACKING

SPALLING

still in motion. Watch such a cracked wall carefully. If it's moving quickly, the foundation is unstable and needs immediate attention.

Repairing Mortar. Maintenance on a brick wall should include a careful check of the mortar joints. Any mortar that is loose, spongy, and easily scraped away needs to be repointed. This process includes excavating the mortar to a depth that is no less than the width of the joint, cleaning away all loose dust and debris, and then refilling the joints with mortar. Without repointing, the process of deterioration accelerates, particularly in winter due to freezing and thawing. Water gets into the cracks and expands as it freezes, forcing the cracks to enlarge. You can expect to repoint brick homes built before 1900, but not because of age alone. The mortar commonly used at that time was lime-based, which is softer and very porous.

Bricks are generally more durable than the surrounding mortar, although leaks and condensation can sometimes harm them unexpectedly. Water absorption through the brick can lead to fragmentation and flaking of the brick face. To avoid the potential problems associated with this splitting action, called spalling, keep water out of your masonry walls, and repair leak-prone brick and mortar joints as soon as possible.

CLEANING BRICK

Sandblasting and power washing are effective cleaning techniques. But the force could seriously erode the mortar joints (right), particularly in older buildings. Chemical cleaning (below) may produce good results with less damage. If you want to power-wash brick (bottom right), test the treatment on a small patch of wall using a low-pressure setting (under 700 pounds per square inch). In older buildings, mortar may break away under a more forceful flow. Under high pressures, even some modern brick may begin to pit. In all cases you'll need to protect nearby shrubs and flowers with drop cloths or plastic sheeting.

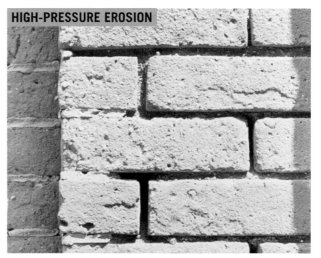
HIGH-PRESSURE EROSION

CHEMICAL CLEANING

POWER WASH

CHAPTER 6 Brick

Cleaning and Repairing Walls

There are four basic ways to clean masonry: by sandblasting or using chemicals, steam, or water. Sandblasting takes away surface and embedded dirt—and often some of the masonry, too. Chemical- and steam-cleaning contractors can tailor their mix of chemicals to the job at hand, such as removing algae. Be careful when working with acid cleaners. Water cleaning is a job you can do yourself, either with a bucket and brush or with a pressurized sprayer (power washing).

Plant life can be destructive to brick walls. When ivy roots start growing into cracks in mortar joints, you should cut them as close to the wall as possible and treat the ends with ammonium phosphate paste to kill the plant. Mold and mildew may also take hold on masonry that is not exposed to enough sunlight. To test discoloration, drop a small amount of bleach on the area. It will whiten mildew and have no effect on dirt. To clear the mildew, scrub the area with a solution of one part bleach to one part warm water, and then rinse.

Stains from iron can be removed with a solution of oxalic acid. Mix about 1 pound of the crystals in a gallon of water with ½ pound of ammonium bifluoride. Brush the mix over the stained area, and then rinse. Brick may also become stained with asphalt and tar from a roof. Scrape off as much tar as possible and clean remaining stains with a solvent such as benzene.

Spot Repairs

Fix cracks in brick as quickly as you detect them. Even small cracks in the mortar joints will let water seep into the underlying structure, where it can eventually cause damage. Over time, water and the winter freeze-thaw cycles will turn minor cracks into major problems that are more difficult and expensive to fix.

In some cases you can add fresh mortar over the old. But you'll get better results by digging out old mortar and replacing it in a process called tuck pointing. You can chip it out with a hammer and cold chisel or use a grinder. If the mortar is badly eroded you can simply scrape it out with a nail, hammer claw, or screwdriver.

After you clear old mortar, sweep the joints

REMOVING STAINS

o remove surface stains, start by trying to lift, scrape, slice or shave off the deposit. You'll find that most cleaning agents generally spread the discoloration over a larger area as they dilute stains. Eventually they may release enough material so that you can rinse or wipe away the problem. But sometimes cleaning can create more problems than it solves. To limit the work area, mix cleaners into a paste with diatomaceous earth (pool filter medium), which keeps the cleaner on the wall. The mixture can pull stains from masonry.

STAIN	SOLUTION
Oil	For brick, emulsifying agent; also try repeated passes with paper towel, blotting paper, or other absorbant agent to remove traces of oil left in the brick surface
Iron	1 lb. oxalic acid crystals, 1 gal. water, ½ lb. ammonium bifluoride
Paint	2 lbs. TSP to 1 gal. water; also try scraping or peeling deposits
Smoke	Scouring powder with bleach; paste-like mixture of trichlorethylene and talc; or alkali detergents and emulsifying agents

Tuck-Pointing Brick

TOOLS
- Power grinder (or hand scraper)
- Spray bottle
- Hawk
- Narrow jointing trowel
- Striking tool (for tooling)

MATERIALS
- Mortar mix

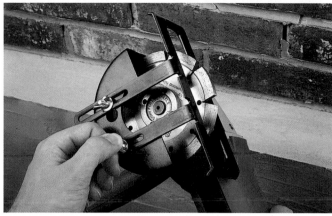

1 *Adjust the depth fence* on a power grinder so that the blade cuts at least ½ in. into the old mortar.

2 *Guide the grinder blade* along the mortar joints. Be sure to wear safety glasses.

3 *Spray the brick and joint* to keep the old mortar from suctioning excess water from the new mix.

4 *Set the new mortar mix* on a hawk next to the joint, and force it in with a thin trowel.

5 *Use a striking tool* to compact the mortar in a concave shape that matches the surrounding joints.

CHAPTER 6 Brick

clean of debris. Then spray a little water in the cavity before forcing in fresh mortar. To minimize cleanup time, set the mortar on a board or mason's hawk, hold it directly against the brick, and push the mortar into place. When the mix starts to set up, tool the joint to match the surrounding seams.

Where the brick itself is cracked or damaged, you will need to replace it. If you shop around, you can usually find replacements for damaged bricks or facing stones that closely match the existing material. Mortar, however, is more difficult to match. You'll probably need to mix a few test batches before you arrive at one that will blend in with the rest of the house. Add powdered colorant, if necessary, to duplicate the existing mortar. Wait for the mortar mix to dry thoroughly, and view the samples outside before making any decisions.

The first step in replacing a broken brick is to chisel it—and the surrounding mortar—out of the wall. After cleaning out the hole and spraying it with water, spread some mortar on the bottom. Then spread mortar on the top and sides of the brick, and slide it into place. Once the wall is sound, you can seal it with a clear silicon-based sealer, which helps the wall shed water and dirt and makes the surface easier to clean.

Replacing Brick

TOOLS
- Work gloves
- 2-lb. hammer
- Cold chisel
- Wire brush
- Trowel
- Striking tool

MATERIALS
- Mortar
- Replacement brick

1 *Any broken* or otherwise damaged bricks will need to be replaced with new ones.

3 *Break away* remaining chunks of mortar, and then wire-brush the surfaces to remove debris.

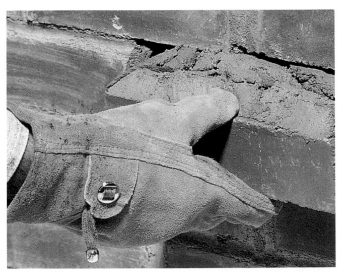

4 *Mix enough mortar* to thoroughly coat the mating surfaces of the replacement brick.

SURFACE DEPOSITS

Efflorescence (left) is a powdery residue caused by water moving through the wall and bringing salts to the surface. But some paints are formulated to shed dirt as the surface breaks down into a powder (right) and washes away slightly with each rainfall. Do not use these chalking paints on siding above a brick wall.

2 *Use a cold chisel* and hammer to chip away the damaged brick, working from the joints in.

5 *Force more mortar* into the joints as needed. Then tool the seams to blend in the repair.

Offset bricks create decorative patterns around fireplaces.

The key part of any dry-laid walk is its base. If you skimp on gravel and sand or skip the crucial compacting steps, whatever you lay on the base will shift. To reduce future maintenance and keep your walkway looking good, remove the sod and dig to undisturbed soil. If you need to remove some large rocks, fill those holes and compact your fill. For small projects and tight spaces, you can use a hand tamper. (See Step 2.)

On larger areas you'll need to rent a gasoline-powered tamper. (See Step 9.) If your walkway is in the path of natural groundwater runoff, it's wise to divert the water. One way to do this is to build a gravel collection trench on the high side of the walkway and run a pipe from it to carry water under the walkway. This extra step can prevent groundwater from gradually eroding the base and undermining the pavers or bricks.

Dry-Laid Paver Walk

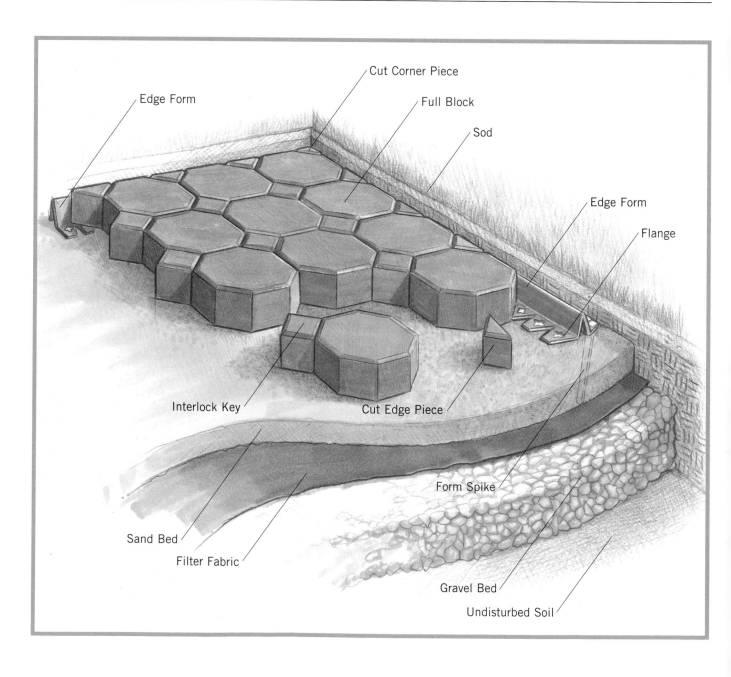

Edge Form
Cut Corner Piece
Full Block
Sod
Edge Form
Flange
Interlock Key
Cut Edge Piece
Form Spike
Sand Bed
Filter Fabric
Gravel Bed
Undisturbed Soil

Dry-Laid Paver Walk Installation

TOOLS

- Work gloves and safety goggles
- Spade (for removing sod)
- Rake or hoe
- Hand or mechanical tamper
- Mallet and bedding board
- Broom
- Water hose
- Ruler and pencil
- Brick set and 2-lb. hammer (for cutting bricks and pavers)

MATERIALS

- Landscape sheeting
- Sand
- Gravel
- Shims or wedges
- Edging material
- Edging spikes
- Exterior-grade pavers
- Lumber for screed board

SMART JOB TIP

You can use redwood, cedar, or pressure-treated wood to keep bricks or pavers from shifting. But this kind of edging requires stakes and can deteriorate in time. Plastic edging is longer lasting, easier to install, and available in segmented lengths that you can bend along the edges of curving walks.

1 *Remove the sod,* and rake out the area to form a uniform base. If you remove large rocks, fill their holes.

2 *After raking out gravel* to form a base of 4 in. minimum, compact it over the entire excavation.

3 *Roll out a layer of landscape sheeting* to suppress weeds and contain the embedding layer of sand.

4 *Spread 1 to 2 in. of sand* over the sheeting, and rake it out to form a roughly uniform base.

CHAPTER 6

Brick

CURVING CORNERS

lastic edging is flexible, but continuous strips are more prone to kink in tight turns than the segmented type (near right), which is flexible enough to edge a serpentine walk. Bear in mind that bricks and pavers have square corners. If you lay out a sharp bend, you'll need to do a lot of cutting. With gradual bends (far right) you can taper the joints and thus need to make fewer cuts.

Drive galvanized spikes to secure flexible edging in a gentle curve.

Gradual curves allow a fan pattern with tapered joints.

5 **Level the sand base** using a screed board. You can set up guides for the screed beside the walkway.

6 **Lay edging along the walkway,** and secure it using long spikes driven through the perforations.

9 **Finish seating the pavers or bricks** by running a power tamper over the surface.

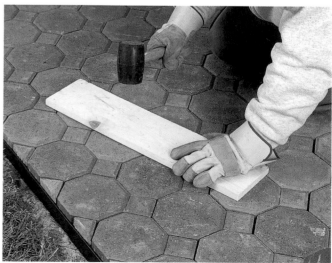

10 **If a paver is still slightly raised,** lay a board on the surface and pound it down with a mallet.

TRIMMING BRICKS

To cut bricks and pavers by hand, mark your cut line, allowing for joint space (near right), and score the line with several taps on a brick set (far right) before delivering a heavy blow to make the cut. You also can use a masonry blade on a circular saw for scoring (wearing eye protection), or rent a wet saw to make many complicated cuts on a large project.

Mark your cut line, allowing for the joint space between units.

Score the full line with taps on a brick set before breaking the brick.

7 **Set the edging to accommodate your pattern,** and start embedding the bricks or pavers.

8 **Work out from the corner,** interlocking pavers and setting them into the sand with a mallet.

11 **Spread fine sand** over the surface, and sweep back and forth to force it into the joints.

12 **Spray the surface with water** to settle the sand, and repeat the last two steps to finish the job.

CHAPTER 6 **Brick**

To build a slab for a small walkway, you may want to mix by hand, always stirring the dry mix before adding any water. But bear in mind that one wheelbarrow-sized batch generally makes less than 3 cubic feet. You would need about nine batches to make just 1 cubic yard. To strengthen the slab, it's important to add a layer of welded wire reinforcement. The wire should run in the center area of the slab. Wires should not protrude from the pour. Accomplish this by rolling out the wire onto half bricks or special mounting hardware called *chairs*. To estimate the amount of concrete you'll need, total up the volume inside the forms in feet, and divide by 27 to convert into the ordering standard of cubic yards. It's wise to build in an excess of about 8 percent by changing the conversion factor from 27 to 25.

Mortar-Laid Walk

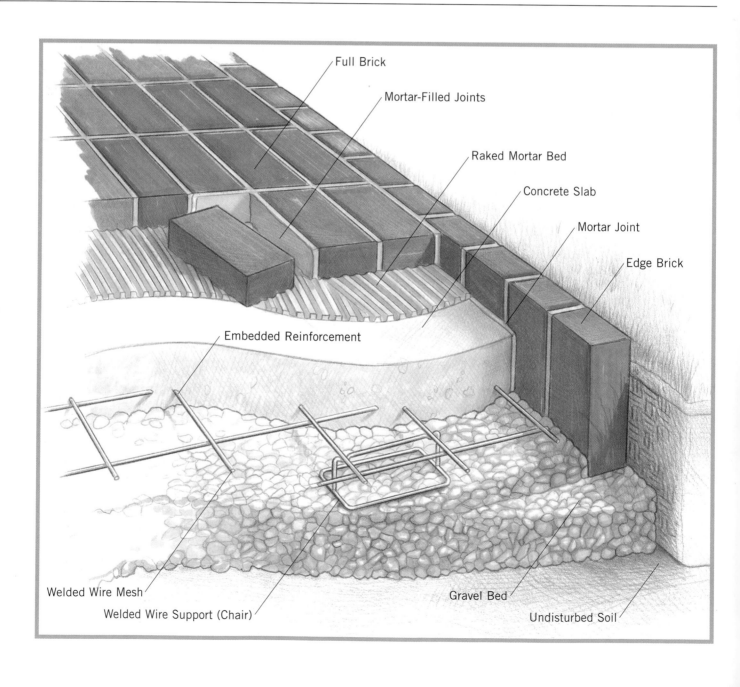

Full Brick

Mortar-Filled Joints

Raked Mortar Bed

Concrete Slab

Mortar Joint

Edge Brick

Embedded Reinforcement

Welded Wire Mesh

Welded Wire Support (Chair)

Gravel Bed

Undisturbed Soil

Mortar-Laid Walk Installation

TOOLS

- Wheelbarrow
- Measuring tape
- Work gloves and safety glasses
- Hammer
- Rake
- Mason's and notched trowels
- Grout bag
- Striking tool
- String and line level

MATERIALS

- Exterior-grade paving bricks
- Reinforcing welded wire
- Gravel
- Lumber for forms and stakes
- Mortar mix
- Concrete mix

SMART JOB TIP

Even a concrete slab reinforced with welded wire can crack if the gravel and ground beneath the slab give way. Prevent this by compacting the bottom of the excavation and the gravel. If the walk area is in a low spot, add a high-side perforated pipe in gravel to divert water.

1 **Measure down** from a level line on stakes to check the level of the excavation at several points.

2 **Rake gravel** over the compacted base of the excavation, creating a base about 4 in. thick.

3 **Build forms** to contain the concrete. Support the boards with stakes driven outside the form.

4 **Lay welded wire** to reinforce the concrete. Support it on wire chairs, as shown, or half bricks.

CHAPTER 6 Brick

EASY-FILL MORTAR JOINTS

Filling joints with wet mortar can be time consuming if you want to keep the brick surface clean and avoid a lot of cleanup work. A faster approach is to sweep dry mix into the joints and then add water. You need to sweep back and forth to thoroughly fill the seams. Then use a fine spray to soak the surface. Too strong a spray can wash out the mortar mix.

Sweep the dry mortar mix into the joints between bricks.

Lightly spray water over the surface, and cover to cure the mortar.

5 *Mix your concrete* by hand in a wheelbarrow or in a rented mixer, or have ready-mix delivered.

6 *Mortar soldier bricks* against the sides of the slab to edge and contain the field bricks.

9 *Set the bricks* in the mortar, using a guide string to keep the courses square and aligned.

10 *Use a grout bag* to force mortar fully into the joints. This device leaves the surface clean.

PROTECTING YOUR YARD

R unning heavy wheelbar-rows full of concrete to your excavation can chop up your lawn and require reseed-ing. To protect the grass and grounds around the work site, you can mix your concrete on a tarp laid in the driveway, and lay a series of planks and plywood sheets along the supply route from your driveway mixing station to the excavation.

Lay boards *as a track for heavy wheelbarrows to preserve the grass.*

7 ***Make a dry layout*** *with the field bricks, placing them in the pattern you have chosen.*

8 ***Trowel out a layer*** *of mortar in an area you can work before it dries. Rake it with a notched trowel.*

11 ***Smooth and compact the mortar*** *between bricks by drawing a striking tool over the joints.*

12 ***Clean any mortar*** *that is forced onto the brick surfaces. Use a mason's trowel.*

CHAPTER 6 Brick

planter can divide sections of your yard, provide a measure of privacy, or create protection around an entrance. You can build planters large or small, rectangular or square, out of the same bricks used on the house or in a contrasting style. This project features the basics you'll need for any situation, starting with a solid concrete footing. Although this straightforward design has only five courses plus a cap, it provides more than enough room for topsoil and plants. And you can vary the details—for instance, by installing shadow-line bricks and various kinds of cap stones. Good drainage is a key component. In a flower pot, the base has holes. In a planter, you can create the same kind of drainage by installing weep tubes in the embedding course of mortar. A base layer of gravel covered with filter fabric also promotes good drainage.

Brick Planter

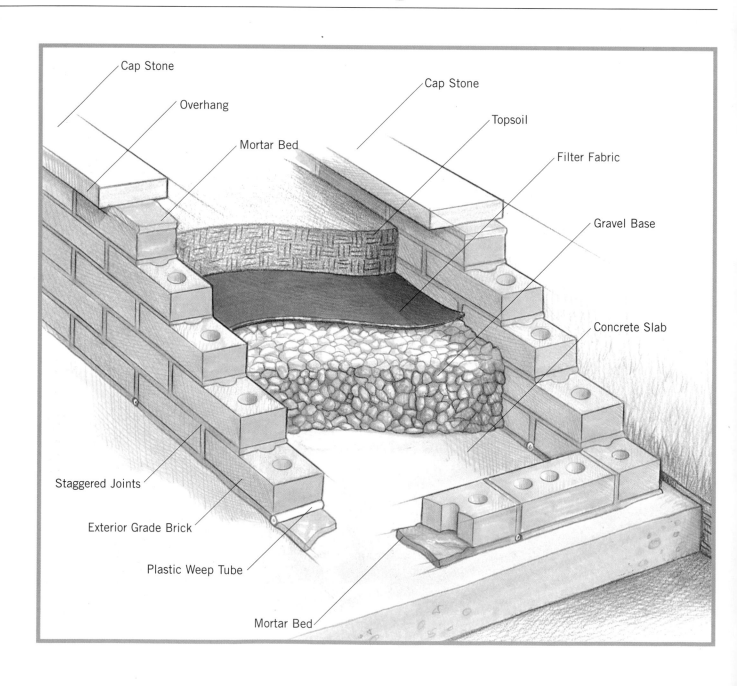

Brick Planter Installation

TOOLS

- ☑ Work gloves
- ☑ Chalk-line box
- ☑ Framing square
- ☑ Mason's trowel
- ☑ Mixing tray
- ☑ Mason's blocks and string
- ☑ Level
- ☑ Striking tool

MATERIALS

- ☑ Bricks
- ☑ Mortar mix
- ☑ Weep-hole tubes
- ☑ Cap blocks

SMART JOB TIP

On oversize planters that hold a large volume of dirt, build in extra strength against hydrostatic pressure by installing reinforcing wire at the corners. If you can't find Z-ties, cut narrow strips from a roll of welded wire or use strips of galvanized mesh.

1 *Snap lines* on the concrete slab or footing to locate the perimeter of your planter.

2 *Use a framing square* to align intersecting chalk lines on the corners of the slab.

3 *Spread an embedding course* of mortar along your chalk lines, and create a furrow with the trowel.

4 *Set the first course* up to the chalk lines, and tap the bricks into level position on the mortar.

CHAPTER 6

Brick

ADDING A FEATURE STRIP

Feature strips can add decoration and detail to the walls of a planter. You can build one or more special courses into the walls, generally near the top, using a contrasting brick. Another option is to offset the feature course, overhanging the main wall by a ½ inch or so to create a shadow line. You can also create patterns with cut bricks turned end-out or set on edge.

A contrasting course of bricks creates a feature strip in the wall.

Create a shadow line by offsetting the bricks by about ½ in.

5 *Install weep-hole tubes* for drainage at every other mortar joint in the embedding mortar.

6 *Butter the ends* of the bricks as you set them in place, compressing the mortar with a trowel.

9 *After leveling each course,* skim the edge of your trowel along the joint to clear excess mortar.

10 *As the mortar firms up,* run a striking tool along the seams to smooth and form the joints.

IMPROVING DRAINAGE

Unless you are installing big bushes or small trees that have a large root ball, you don't have to fill the planter with soil. Instead, you can fill a portion of the space with gravel. To keep the soil above it from clogging the gravel bed and eventually the weep tubes as well, cover the gravel with a double layer of filter fabric. It lets water through but screens out dirt.

Provide drainage *with about 6 in. of gravel covered with filter fabric.*

Cover the fabric *with potting soil or topsoil to hold your plantings.*

7 ***Build up the corners first,*** *and use blocks and strings as a guide to fill in each course.*

8 ***Hold a level*** *against the bricks as you build to be sure that the sides of the planter are plumb.*

11 ***Trowel out an embedding course*** *of mortar for the top cap, creating a center furrow with your trowel.*

12 ***Press the top cap stones*** *into the mortar, and use a level to be sure that they are aligned.*

CHAPTER 6 **Brick**

Y ou can build a real brick veneer wall over a nonmasonry house. But you need to use care with two important parts of the project. First, you need to support the weight of the bricks. Some foundations have a ledge that is wide enough. This ledge transfers the load directly to the foundation and footing and will be adequate in most cases. You also need to attach L-shaped steel wall ties to the solid webs of each block in a concrete-block wall or at about 16-inch intervals in a poured-concrete or wood-frame wall. The second concern is condensation, which must have a way out of the roughly 1-inch-wide gap between the veneer and the house wall. You can provide a route with weep holes (plastic tubes set in the mortar joints) in the bottom two courses. The old system of using rope to transmit water by capillary action generally does not last.

Brick Veneer Half-Wall

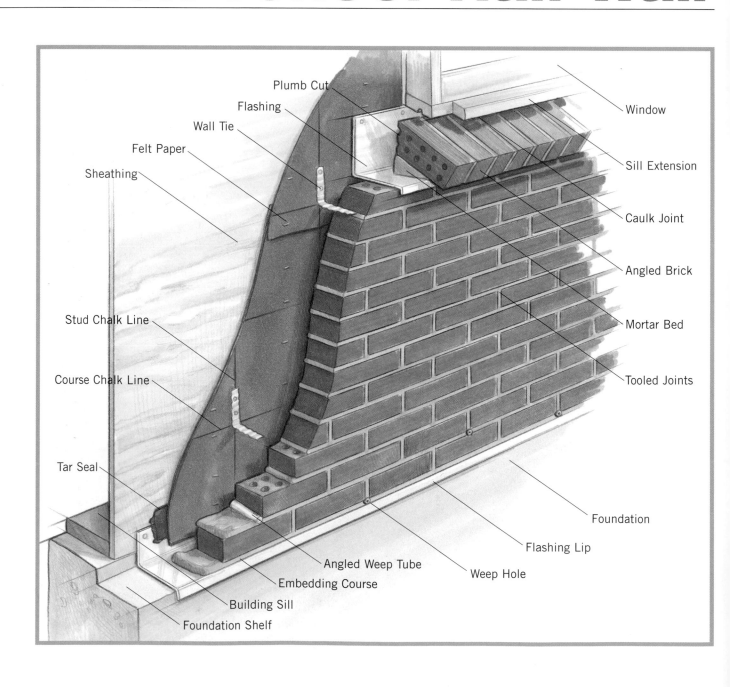

Plumb Cut
Flashing
Wall Tie
Felt Paper
Sheathing
Window
Sill Extension
Caulk Joint
Angled Brick
Mortar Bed
Stud Chalk Line
Course Chalk Line
Tooled Joints
Tar Seal
Foundation
Flashing Lip
Angled Weep Tube
Weep Hole
Embedding Course
Building Sill
Foundation Shelf

Brick Veneer Half-Wall Installation

TOOLS

- Work gloves
- Hammer
- Stapler
- Mason's trowels
- Caulking gun
- Chalk-line box
- String and blocks
- 2- and 4-foot spirit levels
- Jointing tool
- Circular saw with masonry blade

MATERIALS

- Flashing (aluminum or copper)
- Roofing cement
- Felt paper
- Mortar mix and bricks
- Plywood joint spacers
- Weep-hole tubes
- Masonry ties
- Trim for casing extensions
- Caulk
- Roofing nails

SMART JOB TIP

Weep holes in the first course often become clogged with mortar that falls from the backs of joints as you build the wall. You can use plastic mesh to prevent this. (See the feature on page 193.) Another option is to install weep tubes in a staggered pattern in the first two courses of brick.

1 *Set L-shaped flashing* on the foundation ledge, and nail its top to the bottom of the sheathing.

2 *Spread roofing cement* on the top edge of the flashing. Felt paper will cover this seam.

3 *Staple the first layer* of felt paper on the sheathing, so it covers the roofing cement and flashing.

4 *Add a second layer* of felt paper for additional protection of the sheathing and framing.

CHAPTER 6 **Brick**

LAYING BRICKS ON BRACKETS

When the foundation wall does not include a built-in ledge that can support a brick-veneer wall, you can provide support with a steel anchor bracket. Lock the L-shaped length of steel to the wall with lag screws and masonry anchors. Drill pilot holes just slightly larger than the masonry anchors into the solid webs of blocks (or into solid concrete).

Drill pilot holes in the block, and insert masonry anchors.

Drive lag screws into the anchors to fasten the bracket to the block wall.

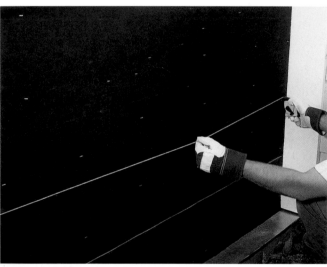

5 *Snap level chalk lines* on the felt paper to mark the height of every fourth course of bricks.

6 *Mark stud locations* by snapping chalk lines every 16 in. on center along the wall.

9 *Butter one end of each brick* with mortar before setting it. Maintain alignment using a string line.

10 *Insert a plastic weep-hole tube* into the joint of every third brick in the first two courses.

USING VENTILATING MESH

Plastic mesh is normally used to provide a ventilating airspace under wooden roof shingles. You can also use it behind the lower courses of a brick veneer wall to keep weep holes unclogged. Mortar falling behind the wall as you work would otherwise block the weep holes. With the mesh installed, excess mortar is caught above the weep holes.

Cut the plastic mesh to length using scissors or shears.

Staple the mesh in the airspace between the brick and the house.

7 *Test-fit the first course* of bricks using strips of ⅜-in. plywood as mortar-joint spacers.

8 *Trowel a layer of mortar* over the flashing to receive the first course of bricks.

11 *Nail masonry ties* into alternate studs every few courses to hold the bricks to the framed wall.

12 *Bend the ties,* and embed the ends in mortar joints as you lay brick to the string line.

CHAPTER 6 **Brick**

EXTENDING A WINDOWSILL

Add rowlock brick under a window, and the installation will not look right (or have the necessary weather protection) unless you extend the sill. To add to the sill, measure the angle at its outer edge and rip a new piece of the same thickness with a matching angle. Sand the existing edge; fasten the new piece using glue and finishing nails; and sand the seam.

Rip an extension for the windowsill to match the existing angle.

Glue and nail the extension in place. Sand and paint to finish.

13 **Check for plumb** every few courses to be sure that the wall is vertical.

14 **Also check for level** every few courses, even if you lay each course to a level string line.

17 **Lay a thin bed of mortar** for the rowlock bricks. They will rest at an angle along the top course.

18 **Butter one face** of each rowlock brick before setting it. The overhang should be about 2 in.

USING A STORY POLE

here are many ways to keep the work level and plumb. You can check periodically with a level, and lay bricks to a level guideline. But it's also helpful to use a story pole. You can make one from a straight 1x4 with clear layout lines showing both the brick courses and mortar joints. You just set the board against the wall to check your work.

Mark off the widths of bricks (on edge) and mortar joints.

Check your work by resting the story pole against the wall.

15 **Install L-shaped flashing** under windows to help keep water from penetrating the wall.

16 **Make a plumb cut** at the top of each rowlock brick so that it will rest against the sheathing.

19 **Tool all joints** before they have cured to smooth the mortar so that the joints shed water.

20 **Caulk the joint** between the windowsill and the bricks. Add trim to cover the siding seam.

CHAPTER 6 **Brick**

Gallery Brick

Brick is one of the most versatile masonry materials. It is used for house walls to provide great strength and resistance to fire, rot, and other elements that can gradually erode wood-frame buildings. There are also many varieties that you can use for walks, drives, and garden walls.

Brick presents a traditional-style wall surface, even in more contemporary settings, when exposed inside the house (opposite).

Weathered brickwork with a classic arched opening (right) forms a durable garden wall.

Brick pavers come in many different styles and are able to blend with any landscape (below left).

The hard edges of brickwork (below right) make for an architecturally elegant set of entry steps.

CHAPTER 6 **Brick**

A patio and garden achieve a classic look with the use of red modular brickwork (opposite top).

Although uncommon, brick can be used as an indoor flooring material (opposite bottom left).

Brick is a good choice for a fireplace mantle. It can either serve as a subtle detail in a room, or it can become a dominant design feature (opposite bottom right).

Face brick is durable and weather resistant, making it a good building material for a fountain (above).

A brick floorplan complements the lush greenery and adds an earthy quality to a shady garden patio (right).

Stone

Materials and Patterns

Cutting and Shaping

Setting and Finishing

Maintenance and Repair

Projects

CHAPTER **7**

Materials and Patterns

Building with stone can be both the hardest and most satisfying project a homeowner can undertake. You need to be in good physical condition and lift stones carefully to protect your back. There's no hurry. After all, you are building something that will stand for a long time.

Choosing Stone

Although many types of stone are available throughout the country, only a few are suitable for building. Besides being accessible, suitable stones must satisfy certain requirements of strength, hardness, workability, and durability.

◼ **Rubble** wall construction has stones that are irregular in size and shape. Fieldstone is one type of rubble, while quarried rubble comes from fragments left over after stonecutting. Random rubble walls are usually dry-laid but can also be mortared.

Coursed rubble walls have a neater appearance than random rubble walls but are more difficult to construct and require a large selection of stone. Rubble stones can also be roughly squared with a brick hammer to fit more easily. Coursed rubble walls can be used for foundations as well as garden and retaining walls.

Mosaic is a tighter version of a random rubble wall. Large and smaller stones are fitted together tightly. To ensure that all of the pieces fit without large gaps, the stones are first laid out on the ground, face down, and test-fitted in the order in which they will be installed.

◼ **Ashlar** is quarry cut to produce smooth, flat bedding surfaces that stack easily. It is generally cut into small rectangles with sawed or dressed faces. Ashlar patterns are not really random, and as with brick, a variety of bond patterns are used: coursed, random, and combination.

Coursed ashlar has a formal appearance and requires precisely cut stone. Ashlar mortar joints are sometimes used as a decorative element in the overall pattern. They may be colored to complement the stone, raked concave like block joints, or filled and dressed to stand out from the face of the wall.

STONE PATTERNS

RANDOM RUBBLE

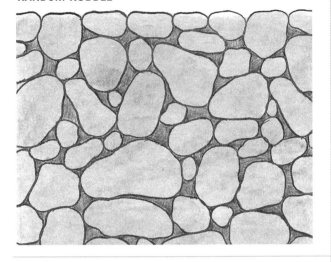

COURSED ASHLAR

COURSED RUBBLE

RANDOM ASHLAR

MOSAIC RUBBLE

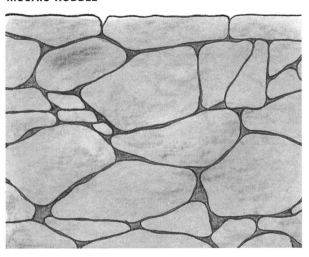

COMBINATION ASHLAR

CHAPTER 7 Stone

Estimating Materials

To estimate how many cubic yards of stone you will need, multiply the length of your wall times the height times the width in feet to get cubic feet, and divide by 27 to get cubic yards. If you are using ashlar stone, add about 10 percent to your order for breakage and waste. If you are using rubble stone, add at least 25 percent. Waste depends a lot on how you plan the layout.

To estimate flagstone for a patio or walk, figure the square footage by multiplying the length times the width. The stone supplier will be able to tell you how much stone you will need based on this figure.

Special Stone Tools

For cutting and shaping stone, you'll need a small sledgehammer that is tempered to strike metal tools safely. A compact, short-handled 2-pound hammer works well. A brick hammer is helpful for chipping off small pieces of rock. A stonemason's hammer is similar to a brick hammer but heavier with a broader edge. A rubber mallet is used to seat flagstones in sand. Stone chisels, available with differently shaped heads, are used to break stones. To lay out stone walls, patios, or walks you'll need wood stakes, mason's twine, and a spade.

Planning can produce interlocked walls where stones form part of the face and the top at the same time.

Common Types of Building Stone

Bluestone: uniform and dense; used for caps and hearths.

Limestone: soft and workable in light grays and tans.

Rubble: irregular shapes, sizes, and colors of fieldstone.

Flagstone: quarried into paving slabs ½ to 2 in. thick.

Synthetic Stone: manufactured in regular widths.

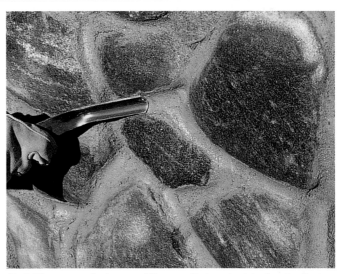

Cut Stone: real stone with one flat-cut side for facing.

CHAPTER 7 Stone

Cutting and Shaping

Working with uniform sizes is one way to eliminate the toughest part of working with stone: cutting it. This is a job you want to do as little as possible because it is difficult, time consuming, and easy to get wrong with a hammer blow that breaks a stone in the wrong place.

If you use irregular shapes and sizes, some cutting and trimming will almost always be necessary. But you can minimize cutting with good planning and careful selection of compatible stones. It pays to make a complete dry layout of a flagstone walkway, for example, trying different combinations of shapes and sizes that nestle together with a minimum of trimming.

Cutting Stone

When you are laying stone in mortar, you often can hide slightly irregular shapes by burying them in the mortar joints. When you are laying stones dry, without mortar, the fit of the stones usually must be more precise both for aesthetics and stability. For both types of stonework though, you will often have to cut and shape individual stones to make them fit better. Whenever you are cutting stone, be sure to wear heavy leather gloves and safety goggles.

While granite is difficult to cut, limestone, sandstone, and slate are relatively easy to work with once you get the knack. First, position the stone on solid ground for firm, even support. Do not lay the stone on concrete because the hard concrete surface may cause the stone to break in the wrong place. The job will be easier (and safer) if you build a small sand box, as shown below. Even a shallow bed of sand can support irregular shapes while you score cut lines and break stones to fit your layout.

You can mark the cutting line with chalk, a pencil, or a scratch awl. Then use a hardened stone chisel to score the cut by positioning the blade of the chisel along the intended line and tapping lightly with a hammer.

You need to move the chisel along the scored line as you strike with a heavy hammer or mallet. In most cases, you'll need to cover the same ground again, setting the chisel in the groove and gradually making the score line deeper.

Sometimes a stone will break along the line before you have scored it all the way. This is a tricky part of the process. For some stones light hammer blows will score a line; for others, you'll need heavier blows.

Once the score line is complete, strike one sharp blow to break the stone. It helps to position the stone with the score line over a pipe or narrow strip of wood that serves as a fulcrum. Remove any small bumps or protrusions with a point chisel, placing the point at the base of the bump and tapping with the hammer.

Cutting Flagstone

1 *If you have many stones to trim,* build a small sand box in which you can nestle irregular stones.

2 *Score the stone* along your mark with a stone chisel, tapping firmly with a 2-lb. hammer.

A classic rubblestone chimney column can be the centerpiece of any room, even if it's not a log cabin.

3 **After scoring the line several times,** *insert a pipe or narrow board under the score line.*

4 **The pipe provides a fulcrum** *that helps the stone break cleanly when you strike it.*

HAND CUTTING TOOLS

Traditional stonecutting tools generally are larger and heavier-duty than standard do-it-yourself models. Aside from protective equipment, including gloves and safety glasses, hardened steel splitting chisels are used for starting drill holes and cleaning up the sometimes ragged edges along split lines (far right). Stone hammers generally weight at least 2 lbs.

Heavy-duty stone tools *include chisels and a heavy hammer.*

Hardened steel chisels *are used to clean up edges of split stone.*

Traditional Stone Cutting

TOOLS

- Ruler and chalk-line box
- 2-lb. hammer and stone chisel
- Power drill and masonry bit
- Wedges and shims (called feathers)

MATERIALS

- Large pieces of hard stone, such as granite

1 ***Strike a chalk line*** *along the length of the stone where you want to split or trim it.*

4 ***Insert a steel wedge*** *in each hole surrounded by a pair of steel shims, called feathers.*

5 ***Tap on each wedge in turn*** *until it seats. You'll feel and hear a solid sound as the wedge seats.*

POWER CUTTING TOOLS

Professional stone masons often use air power to speed up the process of splitting and trimming. This requires a compressor (near right) to supply pneumatic power and a special driver head that holds the tools (far right). Controlling the jackhammer action supplied to the various chisel and shaper tools requires a good deal of strength aside from experience.

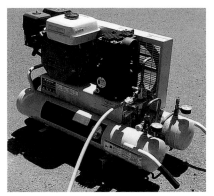

A compresser supplies pressurized air to drive tools.

An air hose is connected to a driver head that holds the tools.

2 *Make starter points* for the drill bit with a hammer and blunt-pointed cold chisel.

3 *Use a powerful ½-in. drill* with a masonry bit to drill holes about as deep as the wedges.

6 *Continue tapping each wedge* in turn with one or two blows until the stone starts to crack.

7 *A few final blows* on the tightest and highest wedges should split the stone completely.

CHAPTER 7 **Stone**

Setting and Finishing

There are many ways to set stone. The method most often depends on the material you are working with and the type of installation. There are many possibilities because stone can be used on paths and patios, as free-standing walls, or as facing material against another structure.

Stone in Sand

On walkways and patios, setting stone in a bed of sand is the most practical approach. You do need to compact the base, but you don't need to pour a concrete slab. The drawback is that a sand base will shift over time. Generally, use a 2- to 3-inch bed for stones of the same thickness but a thicker bed for stones of varying thickness.

Screed a sand bed using a straight 2x4 with the ends riding on guides to keep the sand surface uniform. The guides can be forms built around the work area and secured with stakes once they are level with each other. You can also embed pipes in the sand, use them as screeds, and fill in the shallow troughs with more sand after you remove them.

Embed stones in the sand bed with firm taps of a rubber mallet. Finish by sweeping sand

Setting Manufactured Face Stone

TOOLS
- Mixing tools and mortar box
- Layout string and level
- Trowel and hawk
- Jointing tool

MATERIALS
- Mortar mix
- Face stone

1 *Manufactured face stone* is thinner and lighter than full stone and pressed into the mortar bed.

2 *Check courses with a level,* as stones are slightly irregular to create a less manufactured look.

3 *After embedding all the stones,* fill the joints between courses with mortar, and tool to finish.

Solid fieldstone walls can create graceful terraces and dividers between flat and sloping ground.

Setting Uncut Fieldstone

TOOLS
- Mixing tools and mortar box
- Layout strings and level
- Sledgehammer and brick set
- Trowels

MATERIALS
- Mortar mix
- Rubble (for core)
- Stone

1 *Plan the layout* using the largest square-edge rocks at corners and flat-faced rocks on the sides.

2 *Keep irregular stone faces* to the inside of the wall, and fill the core with rubble.

3 *Mortar the core* after binding the rocks together with an embedding coat on the foundation.

CHAPTER 7 Stone

between the joints with a stiff broom, working a 5- or 6-foot section at a time. A light spray of water will pack down the sand and wash it off the surface. Allow the surface to dry, and repeat the process until all the joints are filled and compacted. You'll probably need to replenish the sand periodically, usually once a year.

Stone in Mortar

Using mortar is the more solid but more difficult way to build with stone. You can certainly set one piece on top of another and dry-lay a wall the way traditional walls around farm fields are built. But those walls need regular repair. On freestanding garden walls, it's wise to taper the sides in toward the top and to rest the wall on a footing as thick as the wall and twice as wide. Or you can build on compacted gravel, although a heavy stone wall is likely to settle and require maintenance.

On walkways, you can pour a 3- to 4-inch slab over a compacted gravel subbase and embed the stones in the concrete. The joints between stones are typically filled with mortar.

You can also set stone in mortar as facing material—for instance, adding a facade to a foundation wall. You can buy cut stone with one flat surface or use manufactured synthetic stone.

DURABLE DESIGN GUIDELINES

Protective Cap

Tapered Sides

Tooled Joints

Wider Base

Twice Wall Width

Equal to Wall Thickness

½" Rebar

Concrete Footing

Tip Cutting Stone

You can cut relatively thin stone with a circular saw fitted with a masonry blade. Another option is to score the stone with a blade cut before finishing the cut by hand. This can help you get a clean edge. To cut by hand, mark your cut line across the stone and score it with a stone chisel and hammer, working back and forth. With the score line etched into the surface, place a board or pipe under the stone for leverage and use heavier hammer blows to break the stone.

The stone chisel scores the surface, and heavier blows with a 2-lb. hammer break the stone.

Laying Stone Pavers

TOOLS
- Shovel, rake, and tamper
- Layout string and level
- Hammer and cold chisel
- Broom and garden hose

MATERIALS
- Plastic sheeting
- Sand and gravel
- Pavers
- Screed boards or pipes

1 *Embedded pipes* serve as screeds for a straight board that you pull along to level the sand base.

2 *Use string guides* to layout the stones. Set them firmly in the sand using a rubber mallet.

3 *Check the surface* with a level; run a straightedge across the seams to find and correct high spots.

4 *Brush sand across the surface,* working your broom back and forth to fill the joints.

5 *Spray the surface with water,* and brush on another layer of sand until the joints are full.

CHAPTER 7 Stone

Maintenance and Repair

Properly laid on a solid footing, stone structures should last indefinitely. They don't, due to the weak link—the mortar joints. Various stresses can cause small cracks and slight crumbling that are the skin-deep indicators of deeper problems to come, unless you repoint—the term for cleaning out and replacing deteriorated mortar joints.

Once mortar joints are cracked, water can seep in, which erodes the wall even more. In winter, of course, the water freezes up and causes much more damage.

You can check joints by eye and with a screwdriver to find sections that are loose or spongy. Don't worry about every hairline crack. The key is to have a sound foundation for new mortar—no matter how deep you have to dig to find it. In some areas you may need to pry out loose chunks that extend well under the stone.

To give new mortar a good bite in the wall, old joints should be excavated at least as deep as the joint is wide—preferably twice as deep. Once the joint is clean, simply pack in fresh mortar and smooth out its surface (a process called tooling), normally with a slight concave shape to match surrounding joints. During this process

COMMON PROBLEMS IN STONE WALLS

Stacked seams in several courses of stone create weak spots that often need repointing.

The lack of tie stones bridging the seam between a wall and a pillar creates a weak link and open seams.

Cracked concrete caps designed to shed water off a wall expose the joints underneath to erosion.

Mortar erosion in large joints causes heavy stones to settle, which can undermine a wall.

you may want to insert a small piece of stone to support any major stone that has settled due to the mortar erosion. You can also use small wooden wedges cut to just the right shape. Once the mortar sets up, simply remove them and fill in the small holes.

Different Cleaning Procedures

There are four basic ways to clean large expanses of stone: by sandblasting and by using chemicals, steam, or water. All are big projects, generally for contractors.

■ **Sandblasting.** An abrasive sandblast treatment is the equivalent of sanding a wood floor. It takes away surface and embedded dirt—and often some of the masonry, too. You need to test the pressure and abrasion on any soft stone.

■ **Chemical Cleaning.** Contractors can tailor a mix of chemicals according to job conditions—for example, to remove algae, oil, or other staining. The structure may do better this way, but, in some cases, surrounding vegetation may not. Some mixes can require a lot of set up time to mask and protect plants, soil, and wood trim on buildings.

■ **Steam Cleaning.** Steam can remove embedded dirt without the risks posed by sandblasting (because it's not abrasive) and chemical cleaning

Repointing Cracked Stone Walls

TOOLS
■ Hammer
■ Stone chisel
■ Trowel
■ Striking tool
■ Whiskbroom or brush
  to clean joints
■ Safety glasses and work gloves

MATERIALS
■ Mortar mix

1 **Chip out loose mortar** using a 2-lb. hammer and stone chisel. Then brush the joints free of debris.

2 **Push fresh mortar** fully into the joints using a small pointed trowel, and compress the seams.

3 **Use a striking tool** (or the handle of any implement that fits) to firm and smooth the seams.

(because it's not caustic—merely burning hot).

■ **Water Cleaning.** Combined with a cleaner, such as a mild solution of muriatic acid, washing and rinsing can clear surface dirt. You can also use a pressure-washer, testing first to be sure the spray does not erode the mortar joints.

Dealing with Stains

Stains from iron and steel hardware, such as shutter hinges, can be scrubbed away using oxalic acid and water. (Always observe the label cautions of powerful cleaners.)

To deal with mold and mildew, use undiluted household bleach, which you can wash away with a scrub brush. Cutting the bleach with an equal amount of warm water should be strong enough to cure mild deposits over a larger area.

On older homes with roofs that have needed repairs, tar may have dripped through old leaks or gutter seams and lodged on the masonry below. Tar will clean up with a solvent such as benzene. But instead of using a solvent that may spread the stain, use a razor knife to cut away almost all of the deposit before cleaning. If an embedded stain remains, which is likely, make a soupy mix of benzene and a binder such as sawdust and pat it in place at least overnight. This mixture will draw out more of the stain.

Stone is a versatile building material that is suitable for garden walls, steps, and house walls.

CLEANING STONE

Washing with water and a mild, over-the-counter solution of muriatic acid is effective on surface dirt and embedded mortar dust. You should always check the results ahead of time by cleaning a small section. Washing with very hard water may leave traces of mineral deposits. Masonry often has enough variation to camouflage minor discolorations.

Wash the wall, and let it dry before applying a clear sealer.

FOUR KEYS TO BUILDING STRONG STONE WALLS

MAXIMUM NUMBER OF STAGGERED SEAMS

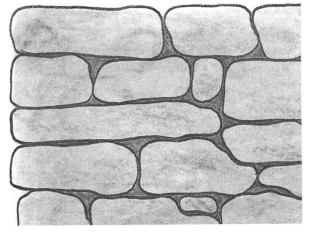

INTERLOCKED CORNERS IN EVERY COURSE

FULL MORTAR BED UNDER CAP STONE

DEADMAN EXTENSION STONES IN RETAINING WALLS

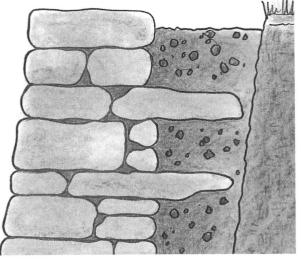

CHAPTER 7 Stone

Dry-laid stone walls generally rest on undisturbed or compacted soil instead of on concrete footings. But you should remove the sod to avoid major settling. If the ground has been graded recently, rent a vibrating compactor to make sure the base is solid. It's also wise to use the largest, flattest stones for the base course and save smaller, more irregular stones for higher courses. To plan the job, you need to lay out your raw materials ahead of time. This time-consuming task will pay off as you gain experience with the stonemason's art of picking the right stone for each location. Although dry-laid walls are meant to look rustic, you will likely need to cut some stone. A hammer and a cold chisel or brick set should serve well enough, although you can score corner stones with a special masonry blade to get straighter cuts.

Dry-Laid Stone Wall

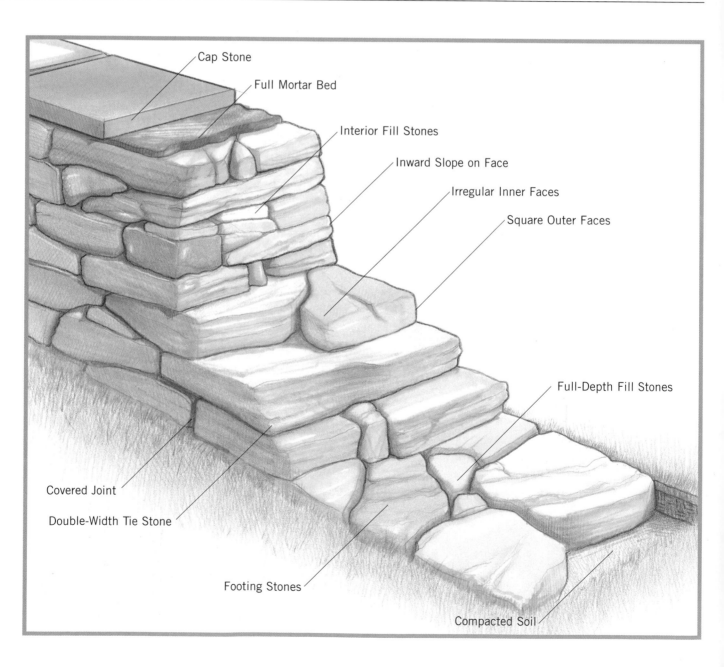

Cap Stone

Full Mortar Bed

Interior Fill Stones

Inward Slope on Face

Irregular Inner Faces

Square Outer Faces

Full-Depth Fill Stones

Covered Joint

Double-Width Tie Stone

Footing Stones

Compacted Soil

Dry-Laid Stone Wall Installation

TOOLS
- Work gloves
- Mason's trowel
- Shovel
- Spirit level
- Hawk
- Mortar box
- Hammer
- Slope gauge (optional)

MATERIALS
- Stones
- Shims or wedges
- Mortar mix
- Cap stones
- Stakes and string

SMART JOB TIP
Stones can be very heavy. Be sure to lift them carefully, keeping your back straight and using your legs to raise the weight. A special back brace or lifting belt will also help to prevent injury during a long day of stonework.

1 *Group your stones* by size and shape, putting aside the largest, flattest stones for the base course.

2 *Mark the wall location* using string and stakes. Then cut along the edges, and roll up the sod.

3 *Dig into the soil base,* if necessary, to nest irregular projections on bottoms of base stones.

4 *Use a flat, double-width stone* to head off both rows in the first course at the end of the wall.

CHAPTER 7 Stone

USING A SLOPE GAUGE

Stone walls should slope inward from bottom to top. The rule of thumb is to factor in about 1 inch of slope per 2 feet of height. You can estimate the slope with a level (Step 9) or make a slope gauge from scrap lumber. This gauge consists of two 1x2s joined at one end and spread apart at the other. With the gauge against the wall, wide end up, the level should read plumb.

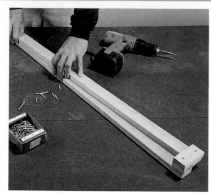

Build the gauge using 1x2s with a spread equal to the wall's slope.

The level reads plumb when the slope gauge rests against the wall.

5 **Fill the interior gaps** between the larger stones with smaller stones and rubble.

6 **Lay the stones** to a guide along the outsides of the wall, with irregular edges facing inward.

9 **Dry-laid stone walls** should slope slightly inward. (See box above to make a slope gauge.)

10 **Use small stones as wedges** to prop up and level larger stones in the course above.

SPECIAL MASONRY BLADES

A hammer and cold chisel can handle most of the cuts on rustic, dry-laid walls. But if you need to make very accurate corner cuts on end stones, for example, you can score the stone with a solid carborundum disk or with a special diamond-carbide tipped blade. Not all of these masonry blades are rated for stone, so you need to check the labels.

Wood blade (top) compared with diamond masonry blade (bottom).

New carborundum blades (bottom) wear down quickly (top).

7 **Use occasional double-wide stones** in the courses that follow to help tie the wall together.

8 **In alternate courses** at the end of the wall, you should install a square-edged cross stone.

11 **Trowel a layer of mortar** over the top course of stones to level and embed the cap stones.

12 **You can use cut stones** with a slight overhang on each side to finish the wall.

CHAPTER 7 Stone

To support a mortared wall you need a solid footing. As a guide, pour a footing that's as deep and about twice as wide as the wall is thick. (For sloped walls, take the average thickness.) Stake the forms to keep their boards from being forced apart by the concrete. Also reinforce the footing with at least two continuous lengths of rebar set in the lower third of the form, several inches in from each side. If the footing turns a corner, bend the rebar to suit and use wire ties at connections, which should be overlapped by about a foot. If the wall will be wide, with a rubble center, you also can set vertical rebar every few feet. On narrower walls this isn't possible because the rebar will keep you from setting and adjusting at least some of the stones. Sort your stones ahead of time by thickness, and set aside double-width stones.

Mortar-Laid Stone Wall

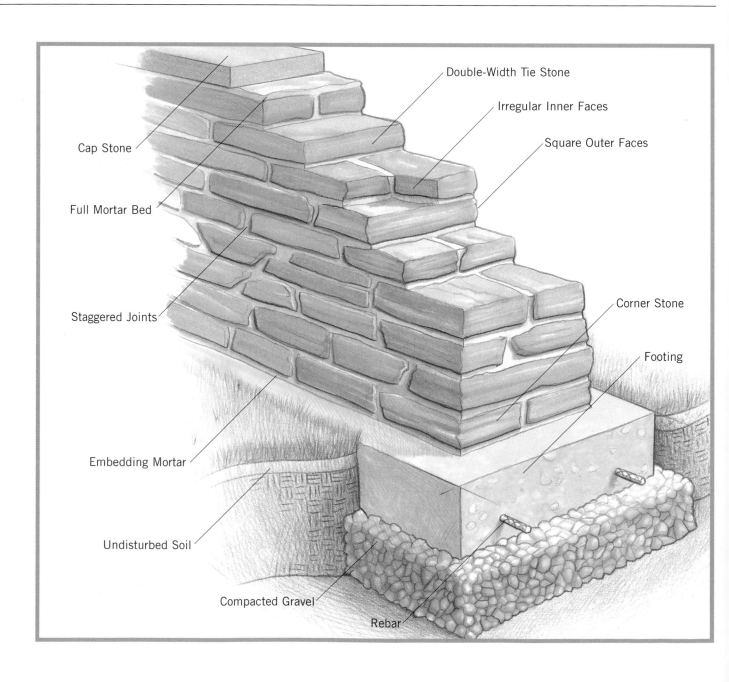

Double-Width Tie Stone

Irregular Inner Faces

Square Outer Faces

Cap Stone

Full Mortar Bed

Corner Stone

Footing

Staggered Joints

Embedding Mortar

Undisturbed Soil

Compacted Gravel

Rebar

Mortar-Laid Stone Wall Installation

TOOLS
- Chalk-line box
- Work gloves
- Trowels
- String and line level
- Whisk broom
- Striking tool
- Mallet
- Level
- Ruler and pencil
- Hose and adjustable spray head

MATERIALS
- Prepared footing
- Stone
- Mortar mix
- Shims or wedges
- 1 x 2 stakes

SMART JOB TIP
Because mortared walls are extremely heavy, you should pour a concrete footing on undisturbed soil. If you excavate after removing sod and loose topsoil, on a slope for example, take the time to compact the base before adding gravel and forms for the pour.

1 **Snap chalk lines** *along each side of the footing to help you align the course of base stones.*

2 **Make a dry layout** *to determine an economical fit, keeping the straightest edges to the outside.*

3 **Trowel a liberal layer of mortar** *up to the guidelines, and embed the first course of stones.*

4 **Use small stones** *or trimmed scrap to fill in the core of the wall between large stones.*

CHAPTER 7

Stone

WEDGING-UP IRREGULAR STONES

Some stones have surfaces that are too irregular to seat properly on the course below. The solution is to temporarily prop them into a level position with one or two small wooden wedges. Wet the wedges (so they will be easier to remove later), insert them, and mortar the joint. When the mortar is firm you can pull out the wedges and fill in the small holes.

Insert wet wooden wedges to temporarily support irregular stones.

Pull the wedges when the mortar firms up. Then fill in the holes.

5 *Drive 1x2 stakes at each end of the wall, and attach a string and line level to guide the courses.*

6 *Build up the corners using full-width stones in every other course to tie the wall together.*

9 *Use a striking tool to smooth and compact the joints into a rain-shedding concave shape.*

10 *Spread a full mortar bed over the top course of full stones and fillers, and then embed the caps.*

USING A GROUT BAG

Pastry chefs use bags to ice cakes, and you can use a larger, heavy-duty version to grout stone walls. This approach helps keep the edges of the stones free of mortar and so reduces cleanup time. Masonry supply outlets sell bags with a variety of nozzles that control the flow. Simply fill the bag with a slightly soupy mix, close the end, and squeeze to apply.

Mix the mortar slightly wet, and trowel it into the bag.

Use the bag like a caulking gun, moving the nozzle as you squeeze.

7 *As your materials permit,* also lay double-wide stones in a staggered pattern throughout the wall.

8 *When the mortar begins to set up,* use a whisk broom to sweep away excess mortar.

11 *Long bluestone caps* on this wall are being tapped level with a rubber mallet.

12 *Wash the wall* with muriatic acid and water (1 to 10 parts), and rinse with a garden hose.

CHAPTER 7 Stone

Facing is a basic masonry application using stone, brick, or other materials to create the appearance of a solid wall that provides structural support. For a stone veneer, you can use synthetic stone or real stone that is selected or split to have flat backs and relatively uniform thickness. Application is straightforward, almost like gluing stones in place. You butter the backs with mortar and press them into a coat of mortar embedded in wire lath reinforcement nailed to the wall. The trick is selecting stones that nestle together like the pieces in a jigsaw puzzle—a mix of large and small, round and rectangular, with seams staggered enough to eliminate continuous vertical joints. On a short foundation wall like this one, you may want to plan ahead and minimize waste by first doing a complete dry layout on the ground.

Facing Stone

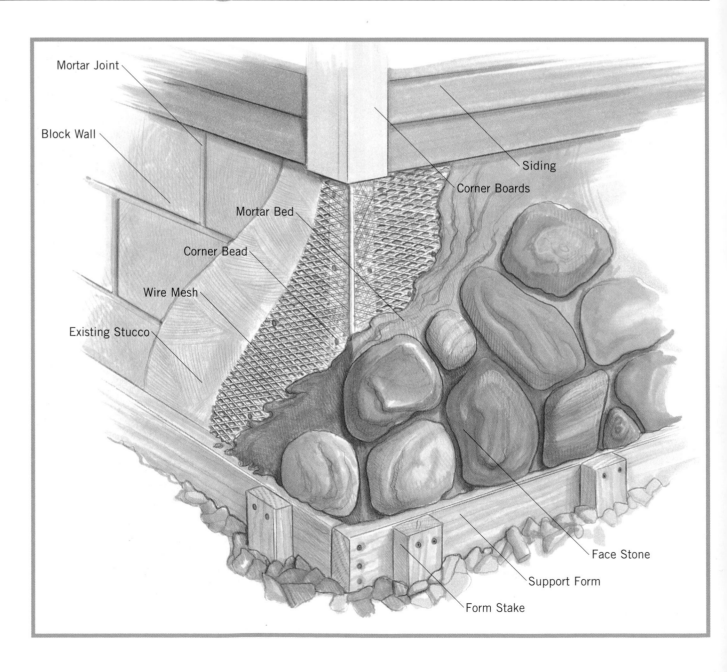

Mortar Joint

Block Wall

Mortar Bed

Corner Bead

Wire Mesh

Existing Stucco

Siding

Corner Boards

Face Stone

Support Form

Form Stake

Stone Veneer Installation

TOOLS

- Work gloves
- Power drill
- Hammer
- Whisk broom
- Striking tool
- Mason's blocks and string
- Mixing tray
- Trowels
- Grout bag

MATERIALS

- Metal lath
- Mortar
- Veneer stone
- 2x4 ledgers
- 1x2 stakes
- Nails
- Screws

SMART JOB TIP

A layer of face stones will cover surface cracks and other cosmetic problems in foundation walls. But if the wall is settling, cracks will disrupt the facing. Old cracks generally have some dirt and debris in them. New or active cracks often are a different color inside than the wall surface.

1 *Install a layer of wire lath* over the old foundation wall, securing it with masonry nails.

2 *Tack temporary base supports* to the wall; level them; and secure them with stakes.

3 *Apply an embedding layer of mortar* to the lath, working the mix fully into the mesh.

4 *Use your trowel to butter* the flat back of the stone with a thin layer of mortar mix.

CHAPTER 7

Stone

TRIMMING STONES

Even when you plan the layout ahead of time, you may need to trim a few stones to achieve the fit you want. If you're short of stones that have a long straight edge for use at the wall's base or top, you can score straight lines with a masonry blade or with a brick set. A small sand box makes a safe work area where you can stabilize even irregular stones.

Score and break irregular stones using a brick set and 2-lb. hammer.

Score straight edges with a masonry blade in a circular saw.

5 *Set the corner stones* with an overlapping stagger to avoid a continuous vertical mortar joint.

6 *Set the base stones* on the level support board, working away from the corner in fresh mortar.

9 *Mix a supply of mortar* to grout the wall. Using a grout bag helps to keep the stone faces clean.

10 *Fill the bag with mortar,* close the end, and apply pressure to force out the grout.

BRACING LARGE STONES

The job would be easier if you used all the big stones on the bottom of the wall and all the little ones on top. But that wouldn't look balanced. To secure a few large stones near the top and keep them from sagging, notch the end of a 1x4, set the notch on the edge of the stone, and angle it down to the ground. You can add a stake to keep the brace from slipping.

Notch the end of a 1x4, and set it on the lower edge of the stone.

Run the 1x4 brace to the ground, and secure it with a stake.

7 *Build up from the base, setting stones to cover the vertical joints in the previous course.*

8 *Check with mason's blocks and string (or a straightedge) to keep the face of the wall flat.*

11 *Use a stiff whisk broom to clear away excess mortar before the grout starts to set.*

12 *Use a striking tool (or even a small spoon) to smooth and shape the mortar joints.*

CHAPTER 7 Stone

lagstone is a traditional and proven material for patios and walkways. It is sold in several thicknesses (generally from 1 to 2 inches) and in muted colors with subtle shadings that help your installation blend with the landscape. There are many ways to lay a flagstone patio and build steps, which is often the most complicated part of the job. The most durable method is to pour a concrete slab and embed the stones in its surface. More often, flagstones are laid in sand on a bed of fine compacted gravel or a mixture of compacted dirt and sand. Sand is useful for screeding to a pitch of about one percent for drainage. Using random shapes is the most challenging approach and creates the greatest waste. You can also use square-cut flagstones designed to fit together in several modular patterns that reduce cutting time.

Flagstone Patio & Steps

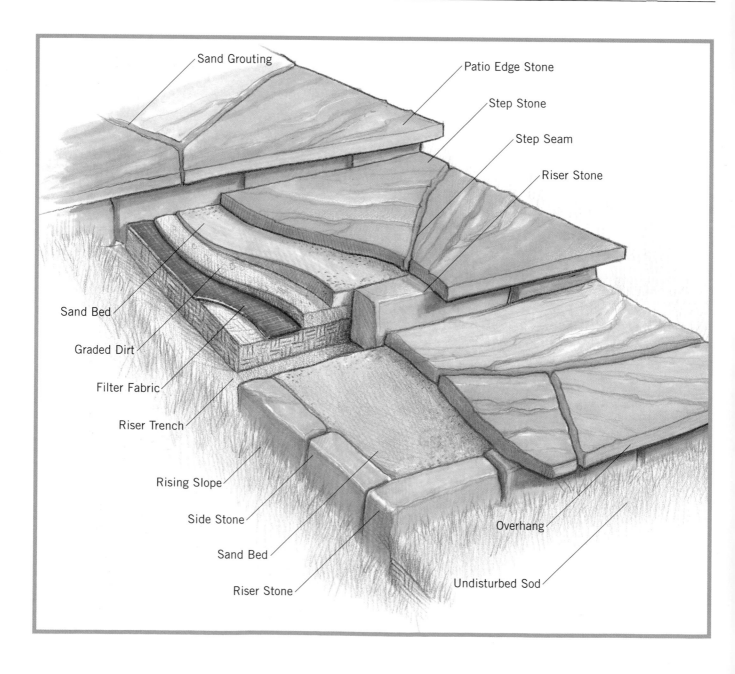

Sand Grouting
Patio Edge Stone
Step Stone
Step Seam
Riser Stone
Sand Bed
Graded Dirt
Filter Fabric
Riser Trench
Rising Slope
Side Stone
Sand Bed
Riser Stone
Overhang
Undisturbed Sod

Flagstone Patio & Steps Installation

TOOLS
- Work gloves
- Shovel and tamper
- Spirit level and measuring tape
- Clamps
- Mortar mixing box
- Mixing hoe
- Hammer
- Rubber mallet and cold chisel
- Push broom
- Garden hose with spray head

MATERIALS
- Stone
- Gravel base
- Filter fabric
- Screeding sand
- Mortar mix
- Stakes and layout string

SMART JOB TIP

To increase the durability of grouted seams between stones you can add cement to the sand before brushing it into cracks. With sand only, you'll have to come back after a day or two to refill the joints that settle after wetting. Another approach is to leave larger gaps, fill with topsoil, and sow grass seed in the seams.

1 *Use stakes and strings to lay out the patio. When the diagonals are equal, the patio is square.*

2 *Dig a shallow trench to embed the edging support stones below the graded patio level.*

3 *Use a hand tamper or the end of a 2x4 to compact the dirt in the bottom of the trench.*

4 *Set the edge stones in the trench so that the tops will be level with the screeded sand of the patio.*

CHAPTER 7 Stone

PLANNING FLAGSTONE TREADS AND RISERS

T he most reliable way to establish the sizes of treads and risers is to stake a long, straight, and level board along the edge of the slope. This allows you to try several combinations. For example, you can extend the treads 18 inches or more to reach a comfortable maximum of 6- or 7-inch risers, or reduce them to achieve a comfortable minimum of about 4-inch risers.

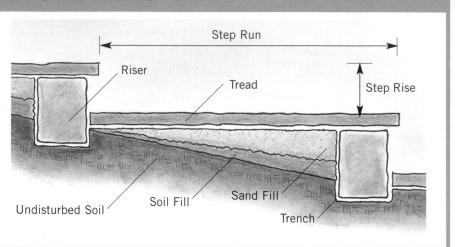

Step Run

Riser

Tread

Step Rise

Undisturbed Soil

Soil Fill

Sand Fill

Trench

5 *Spreading a layer of filter fabric* or black plastic can suppress weed growth through patio joints.

6 *Cover the excavation* with at least 2 in. of sand, and use a straight board to screed the surface.

9 *Set up a level board* to gauge the slope, and lay out the treads and risers of the steps.

10 *Measure down from the level board* at the edge of the tread to establish the step rise.

MOVING STONE

The key to working with heavy stones is leverage. You'll want to move stones with pry bars and dollies instead of with your back, arms, and legs. For clearing and moving large rocks of any kind, consider investing in an oversize pry par, generally called a wrecking bar. A dolly is very handy, considering that a delivered pallet of flagstones weighs about 3,000 pounds.

Wrecking bars are long pry bars that apply exceptional leverage.

A dolly is handy for transporting stones around the worksite.

7 **Set the perimeter flagstones** in the screeded sand, laying the straightest edges to the outside.

8 **Embed flagstones** using a rubber mallet. Check the surface with a straightedge and/or level.

11 **Set up stakes and strings** to mark the treads and guide excavation work on the slope.

12 **Dig a shallow trench** at the outer edge of each tread so that you can embed riser stones.

CHAPTER 7

Stone

PLANNING LAYOUT PATTERNS

A typical delivery of rough flagstones contains many shapes and sizes that are graded by color and width. You can also order cut stones that fit together neatly. With rough material you need to carefully plan the intricate joints on patios and steps. Narrow, sand-filled seams generally require some trimming, while wider seams make greater use of existing shapes.

Consistently narrow joints filled with sand require puzzle-like fit.

Wider, grass-filled joints are easier to plan and create less waste.

13 *Set and level the riser stones* for the steps. You'll need to remove the sod before screeding.

14 *Compact the area behind the risers,* add sand, screed the bed, and check for level.

17 *Embed flagstones* in the sand to form the steps. It's wise to work out the patterns in advance.

18 *You can grout the flagstone joints* with sand or a mix of 4 parts sand and 1 part dry mortar.

SHIMMING A STEP

Even within the standard size categories of 1- and 2-inch flagstone, it's common to find variations of ¼ inch either way. That means one step stone could be up to ½ inch thicker than the next one. Compensate by shimming with flakes of stone. To keep a shim from shifting and the step from sinking, embed the shim in a small mound of mortar.

Check for level, and measure the thickness of the required shim.

Keep the shim stone from shifting by embedding it in mortar.

15 **Follow the same procedures** as you work down the slope, maintaining the tread and riser sizes.

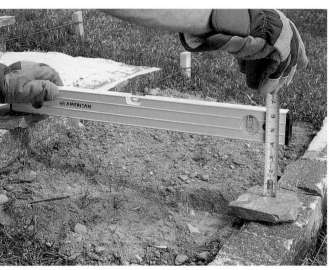
16 **Check the riser stones** by leveling from step to step with scraps of flagstone in place.

19 **Push the sand mix** back and forth across the patio and steps with a broom, filling the joints.

20 **Spray the sand with water,** and refill and respray the joints after the first layer settles.

CHAPTER 7 Stone

Gallery  Stone

Stone is one of the most durable building materials. It's also available in a natural state in more sizes, shapes, textures, and colors than any other material. Use stone to create sweeping walks and drives, and unique garden and retaining walls that blend beautifully with the landscape.

Stonework makes a bold statement in a kitchen (opposite).

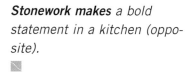

Form a unique wall (top left) by selecting stone in different shapes and sizes.

Stone works well for house and garden walls (above); it blends easily into a design.

Use varying shapes of stone and leave space between pieces for an informal patio (top right).

Stones embedded in sand over a layer of gravel (right) form durable walks and driveways.

With formwork providing support during construction, you can build distinctive arched openings with stone (opposite top left).

A cool bluestone patio (above) offers a sharp contrast to a warm outdoor fireplace.

An extravagant mountainside vista (left) illustrates the many uses of stone; it comprises the patio, the garden retaining walls, and the surface of the balcony.

Get decorative indoors using stone as a flooring material. Mosaics (above right) add a creative touch to any space.

When selecting stone for a design, your options in size and texture are many. A random rubble wall (right) brings historical charm to a sunny setting.

Tile

Materials and Patterns
Preparing Floors
Laying Out the Job
Cutting Tile
Setting Tile
Maintenance and Repair
Projects

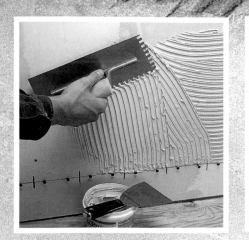

CHAPTER 8

Materials

When most tile is formed, it is fired in a kiln at temperatures ranging from 2000° F to 2500° F. Coatings can be added at different stages for color and decoration, and to protect the tile body. These glazed tiles range from a high gloss to a dull matte finish in a wide variety of colors and patterns. When you visit your tile dealer, you will probably find the ceramic tile selection divided into basic categories of wall, floor, and mosaic tile. There are also many types and sizes of specialty tiles.

Basic Tile Types

Most glazed floor tiles work on countertops and other horizontal surfaces subject to heavy use. Generally, you use glazed floor tiles only on interior floors. Wall tiles are typically thin, lightweight, and porous, so they don't have the strength to stand up to floor traffic.

You can also use sheet-mounted tiles ganged together on a backing of paper, plastic mesh, or fabric mesh. Ceramic mosaic tiles, generally 2 inches square or smaller, are dense-bodied glazed tiles that are suitable for practically any application.

Substrates & Adhesives

You can install tile over smooth-surfaced plywood subflooring or drywall. In bathrooms and kitchens, you may want to install cement backer board. This rigid, portland cement-based panel is designed for use as a substrate, or underlayment, for ceramic tile in wet or dry areas, and is standard in showers and on kitchen counters.

A tile dealer can suggest the best adhesive for the job. The most common and easiest to apply is organic mastic. You simply spread it using a notched trowel. But most organic mastics cannot be used in wet installations or near heat sources. For wet locations, dry-set mortars are sold in powder form and mixed with water. Portland cement mortars, called thinsets, are also nonflammable and water resistant, and are often used over cement backer boards.

K nee pads don't qualify as essential safety equipment, but they can make the job of laying floor tile a little easier. Many professionals use them. But pros work on floors day in and day out, while do-it-yourselfers may tackle this kind of project only once. If you have problems with your knees, by all means use pads. Yet if working on the floor causes you only slight and temporary discomfort, simply roll up a towel, and use it as a cushion. There are several types of pads, both reinforced and padded, that strap on easily to provide a stable working platform.

A—thinset mortar mix; *B*—premixed grouts; *C*—cement backer board; *D*—plywood; *E*—greenboard; *F*—tile mastic; *G*—tile and grout sealer; *H*—tile and grout cleaner; *I*—fiberglass mesh tape; *J*—galvanized screws; *K*—caulking products; *L*—4-mil plastic film (waterproof membrane)

Tile Sizes & Shapes

Field tiles come in several different shapes, including squares, rectangles, hexagons, circles, teardrops, clover leafs, and others. Depending on the manufacturer, the actual size and thickness of these tiles may vary ⅛ inch or so. This is why you can't always mix tiles from different manufacturers.

Single Tiles. Singles are the type of ceramic tile that most do-it-yourselfers use: individual tiles laid one at a time. They are available in a great variety of sizes, colors, and patterns. Most custom decorative and hand-painted tiles fall into this category as well. Single tiles are typically ¼ to ⅜ inch thick and range in size from 1 x 1 inch to 12 x 12 inches square, although larger sizes and different shapes are available.

Sheet-Mounted Tiles. Sheet tiles are evenly spaced tiles mounted on a backing sheet of paper, plastic mesh, or fabric mesh. They may also be joined by small dabs of vinyl, polyurethane, or silicone rubber in a process

called dot-mounting. Many sheets are 12 inches square or larger. With small tiles it's wise to use sheet-mounted applications. Otherwise, it's very time-consuming to set the tiles one by one.

Trim and Specialty Tiles. All tiles that are not placed in the field are referred to as trim tiles. They are used to create smooth, finished edges, turn corners, and create a variety of accents.

■ **Bull-nose** tiles are basically field tiles with one or two curved edges left exposed.

■ **Cove** pieces are used to gently turn corners at a right angle. The corner can turn either inward or outward.

■ **Bases** have a finished top edge and are used where the floor is tiled but the wall isn't.

■ **Beads,** sometimes called quarter rounds, are used to finish off corners and edges. They turn a rounded, 90-degree angle.

■ **Rounds** are trim tiles that create a rounded corner instead of an angular one.

■ **Edgers** are generally L-shaped tiles used mainly on the edges of counters.

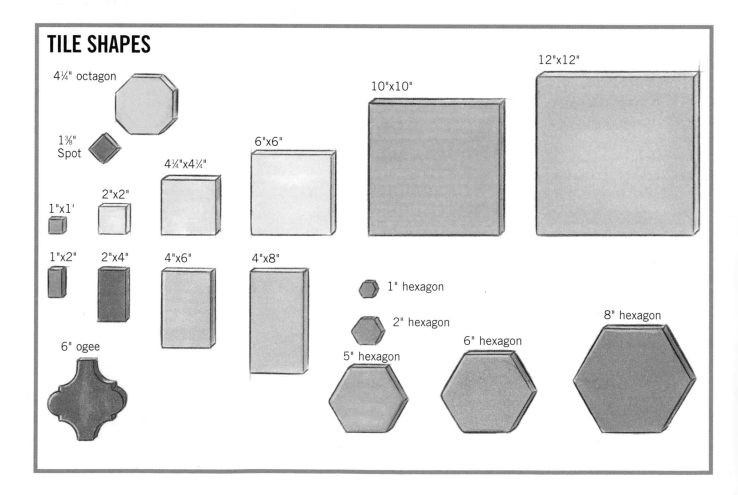

TILE SHAPES

4¼" octagon

1⅜" Spot

4¼"x4¼"

2"x2"

1"x1'

6"x6"

10"x10"

12"x12"

1"x2"   2"x4"   4"x6"   4"x8"

6" ogee

1" hexagon

2" hexagon

5" hexagon   6" hexagon   8" hexagon

BASIC TILE COMBINATIONS

Even when you stick to one size of tile throughout the main field, there are three basic ways to set them on the wall.
Jack-on-Jack (right) aligns the grout joints and stacks one tile directly on top of another.
Running Bond (below left) is a basic brick pattern with the joints staggered from course to course.
Diagonal Jack-on-Jack (below right) is set up just like jack-on-jack but is turned 45 degrees.

TILE CORNERS

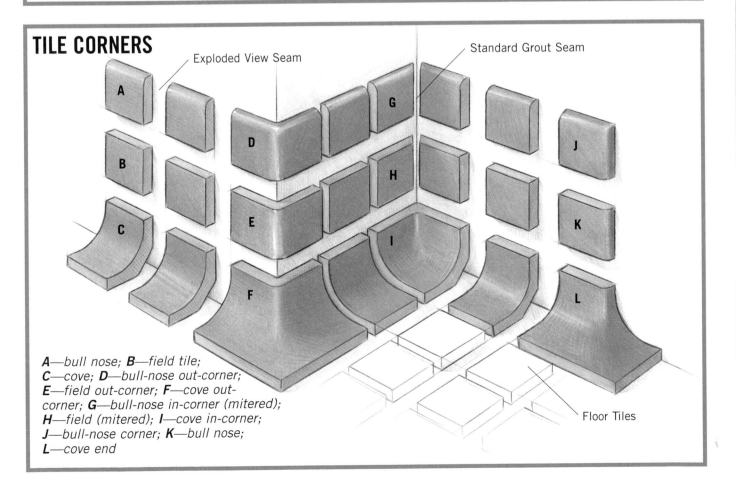

Exploded View Seam

Standard Grout Seam

Floor Tiles

*A—bull nose; **B**—field tile;
C—cove; **D**—bull-nose out-corner;
E—field out-corner; **F**—cove out-
corner; **G**—bull-nose in-corner (mitered);
H—field (mitered); **I**—cove in-corner;
J—bull-nose corner; **K**—bull nose;
L—cove end*

CHAPTER 8 Tile

Tile Patterns

The way you combine the different design elements of shape, size, and color determines the overall pattern of the tile. Consider that the pattern serves not only to add visual interest to the surface but also to underscore particular features of a room. For example, a strong directional pattern can make a room look longer, while a crossing pattern can make a room look wider. A pattern change can also separate spaces—at a pass-through between rooms—whereas a continuing grid can draw rooms together.

Choice of grout has an impact on the design. A contrasting grout color will emphasize a pattern, while a matching grout color will make the pattern recede. Also, because dark grout hides dirt better than a light-colored grout, think twice before using white grout.

Changing the scale or pattern by installing a tile baseboard, for example, can separate wall and floor grids and disguise any discrepancies, as when grout joints don't align. There are many types of special tiles, generally with a cove shape, that suit this purpose. With so many possibilities, it pays to experiment with some of the pattern and color combinations shown below.

BASIC TILE SHAPES AND PATTERNS

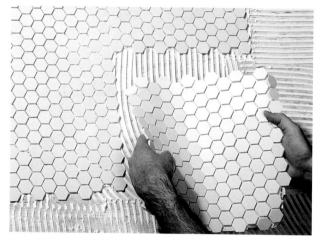

Small hexagonal tiles (and other small units) are sheet-mounted to make installation more convenient.

Rectangular tiles can form various patterns, from straight running bonds to more elaborate basketweaves.

Custom combinations of different sizes, shapes, and colors are possible if you stick to stock sizes.

Sheet-mounted tiles are available in many patterns, including random combinations of color and size.

To support heavy floor tiles, you generally need extra subflooring, and sometimes extra framing as well.

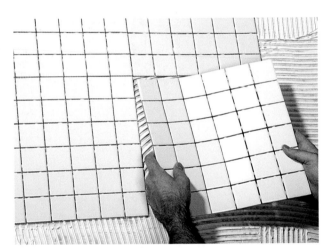

The many variations on a square *include sizes you set individually and the sheet-mounted tile shown.*

By combining basic shapes *such as squares and rectangles, you can create a wide variety of patterns.*

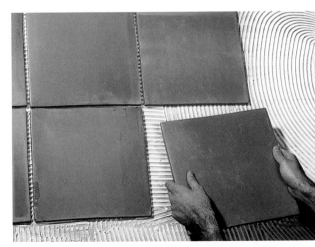

The most basic tile shape *is a square that forms a symmetrical grid, such as this 12x12-in. terra-cotta.*

Hexagonal tile *creates an interlocked, multidirectional pattern that requires edge trimming.*

CHAPTER 8 Tile

Preparing Floors

Tiling is no different from other do-it-yourself projects in one important respect: much of the work lies in the preparation. You can install ceramic tile directly over some existing floor coverings. But most need to be strengthened to eliminate flexing that can crack grout joints. In some houses, you may have to remove the surface flooring, strip some of the subflooring, build up some of the framing, and start from scratch. If you find it too difficult to remove an old floor covering, and it is in bad shape, you may be able to bury it under plywood or a backer-board underlayment that creates a sound surface for tile.

The standard procedure in most cases is to apply an additional layer of ½-inch plywood. But a layer of ¾-inch plywood fastened with glue and screws into the joists is better.

If you are installing a new floor, plan the job to provide extra-strength framing that will remain rigid under tile. For example, if plans call for 2x8s, you can install 2x10s instead. Another option is to stick with the size of joists elsewhere but decrease the spacing from 16 to 12 inches on center. In existing homes, you can strengthen floor frames by doubling joists.

Strengthening Existing Floors

TOOLS
- ◼ Power drill-driver
- ◼ Screwdriver bit
- ◼ 4-foot level

MATERIALS
- ◼ Extra joist
- ◼ Construction adhesive
- ◼ Screws

1 *Driving screws into the joists at 6-in. intervals reduces squeaking and solidifies the floor.*

2 *Locate weak or sagging floor joists by checking across the ends of several joists with a level.*

3 *Strengthen a weak joist by adding a second joist secured with construction adhesive and screws.*

BRIDGING

Bridging connects the joists to each other, mainly to prevent twisting, but also to make the overall frame more solid. Wood bridging is solid pieces of lumber set perpendicularly between the joists and staggered to allow face-nailing. Older systems used smaller pieces of lumber set in an X-shape. In newer houses, bridging is usually metal strapping set in an X-pattern between joists.

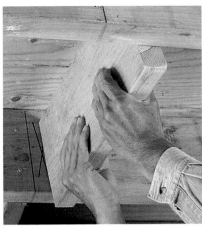

Solid bridging is made of the same lumber as the floor joists.

Strap bridging serves the same purpose and is easier to install.

Adding New Underlayment

TOOLS
- Circular saw
- Power drill-driver
- Screwdriver bit
- Measuring tape
- Chalk-line box

MATERIALS
- Plywood
- Galvanized screws

1 *Cut and install* half sheets so that the new joints are staggered and do not fall on the old joints below.

2 *Set the half sheet* next to a full sheet, but leave at least a ¼-in. gap along the walls.

3 *Snap a chalk line* over the joists, and drive screws long enough to reach into the framing.

CHAPTER 8 Tile

Laying Out the Job

Once you have selected the tile and overall pattern and prepared the floor with underlayment, you need to lay out working lines that will help you position the tiles. In most cases, the most practical plan is to find the center of the room and lay out field tiles that leave equal-sized partial tiles at the edges.

Square-Cornered Room. If the room is square, snap chalk lines that cross in the center. Starting at the intersection, dry-lay a row of tiles along each working line, or use a layout stick to determine where cut tiles are needed and what size they will be. Be sure to account for the widths of grout joints.

Out-of-Square Room. If the room is out of square, align the tile with the most prominent wall, and make irregular cuts as needed against the other walls. To determine which corner is most square, place a tile tightly against the walls in each corner of the room. Project chalk lines from the outside corner of each tile in both directions. Then check the intersections of the chalk lines at each corner for square, and choose the one that is closest to 90 degrees.

Adjoining Room. Divide the area into two sections, and snap the layout lines at 90 degrees.

Diagonal Layout. From the intersection of the original working lines, measure out an equal distance along any three of the lines, and drive a nail at these points. Hook the end of a measuring tape to one of the nails, and hold a pencil against the tape at a distance equal to that between the nails and center point. Use the tape and pencil as a compass to scribe two sets of arcs on the floor. This will provide points along the 45-degree diagonal. Your diagonal lines will line up with grout joints between tiles. Ideally, the original lines that are square in the room should slice through the corners of the tiles. You may need to adjust the working lines to achieve the best pattern of partial tiles at all four walls. When setting the tiles, fill in one quadrant at a time.

FOUR OPTIONS FOR TILE LAYOUT

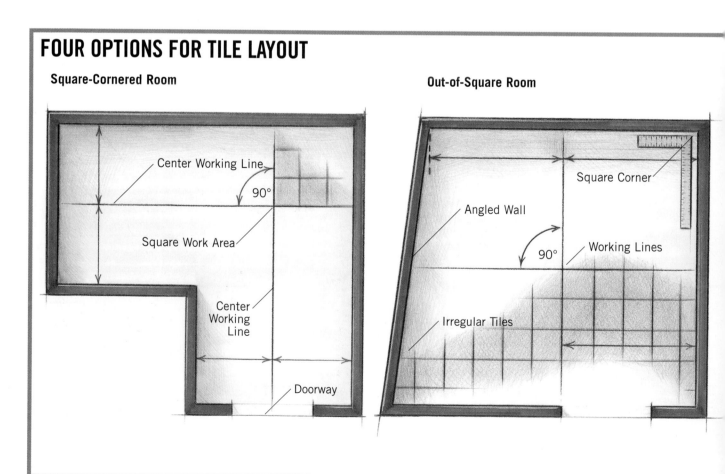

Square-Cornered Room

Center Working Line

90°

Square Work Area

Center Working Line

Doorway

Out-of-Square Room

Square Corner

Angled Wall

90°

Working Lines

Irregular Tiles

Many types of floor tiles, including the quarry tiles shown here, can be used on vertical surfaces as well.

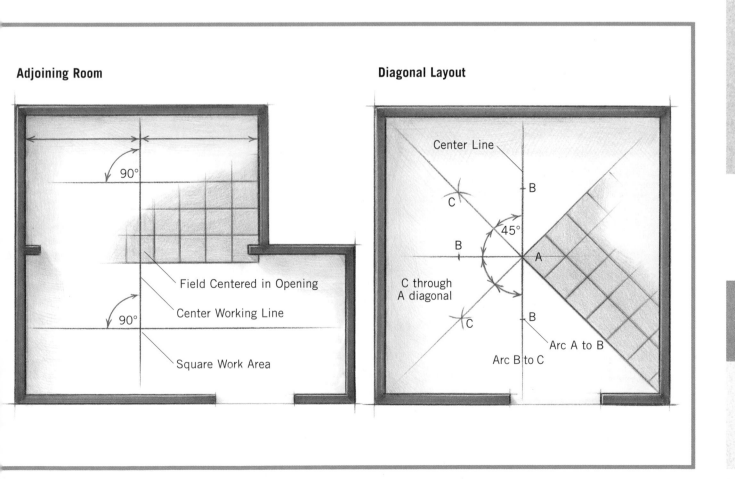

Adjoining Room

90°

90°

Field Centered in Opening

Center Working Line

Square Work Area

Diagonal Layout

Center Line

B

C

45°

B

A

C through
A diagonal

C

B

Arc A to B

Arc B to C

CHAPTER 8

Tile

Cutting Tile

To make straight cuts in thin glazed tile, score the surface with a glass cutter, center the tile over a thin dowel, and press down on both sides to snap it along your score line.

But the tool of choice for most tile projects is a snap cutter. It holds the tile in position as you draw a carbide wheel along a guide rod, ensuring a square cut. Most cutters have a built-in ridge and a handle that you use to snap the tile once it's scored. Most snap cutters will not work on large, thick tiles, such as quarry tile or pavers.

If you have just a few of these tiles to cut, fit a hacksaw with a carbide-grit blade and cut a groove about 1/16 inch deep in the face of the tile. (Very thick tiles may require a second cut on the back to get a clean snap.) Then set the tile over a dowel and press to snap.

If you have many tiles that are difficult to cut in a snap cutter, use a wet saw. This tool is also the best bet (on any kind of tile) if you have many irregular cuts to make. A wet saw is basically a stationary circular saw with a water-cooled carbide-grit blade. (You can rent one for the job.) The saw component stays put, and you guide the tile into it on a sliding table.

You can use cut tiles to create accents and other decorative details.

THREE WAYS TO CUT TILE

TILE NIPPER

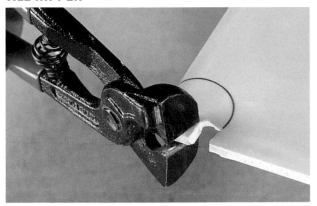 

Take very small bites along the edge of the tile, and gradually work up to your layout lines.

Nippers leave a ragged edge, so where appearances count, clean up this edge with a file.

SNAP CUTTER

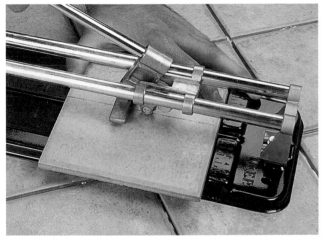 

Set the tile against the stop at the head of the snap cutter, and draw the cutting wheel along the guide.

Push down on the handle, making the tile snap evenly straight along the scored line.

POWER WET SAW

 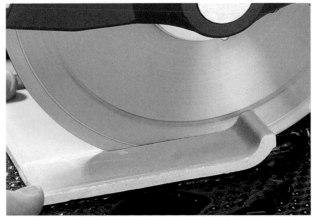

Adjust the sliding fence on the saw table to square up and control the cut, and to size the tile.

The fine-toothed blade is lubricated with water. Although slow, this saw produces a very clean cut.

Setting Floor Tile

To keep the first rows straight, find the center of the room or tile area, and snap chalk lines along the floor to use as guides. Centering creates the largest area of full-sized field tiles and leaves partial tiles around the perimeter.

Spread adhesive up to your guidelines using a notched trowel, but don't apply more adhesive than you can cover with tile before the adhesive skins over (begins drying). The amount of workable area depends both on the working time of the adhesive and on the speed at which you lay the tiles. When you spread the adhesive, use the method and trowel notch size recommended by your tile dealer.

After spreading the adhesive, press a tile into place and twist it slightly to bed it firmly. You can also use a bedding block (a length of 2x4 wrapped in a carpet scrap), sliding the block across the tiled surface while tapping it lightly with a hammer or rubber mallet.

Also check tiles frequently with a layout stick to make sure that they are aligned. You can make small corrections by wiggling the tiles. If a tile sinks below the surface of surrounding tiles, remove it and add more adhesive.

Installing Field Tiles

TOOLS
- Measuring tape
- Notched trowel
- Mallet
- Layout stick
- Chalk-line box
- Pencil

MATERIALS
- Tile spacers
- Tile adhesive
- Tile

1 *A dry layout* takes extra time, but it helps you visualize how the field tiles will fit in the room.

4 *Set tile spacers* to maintain the grid layout. These may need to be removed before grouting.

5 *Check the tile alignment* every few rows or so with a layout stick that accounts for grout joints.

LASER TOOLS

L aser layout tools and levels can be useful when laying tile. Unlike a chalk line, a laser line can be seen even when you accidentally spread adhesive over it. Laser tools come in all shapes and sizes for a number of different applications. Small, battery-powered models are handy because you can rotate them to project different guide lines and to check tile alignment.

2 *Use a notched trowel* that leaves ribs of adhesive to spread up to your guidelines.

3 *Set the tiles* into the adhesive bed. Embed them with moderate pressure for a secure bond.

6 *To mark edge cuts,* set a tile on top of the full edge, and use another tile to mark the margin.

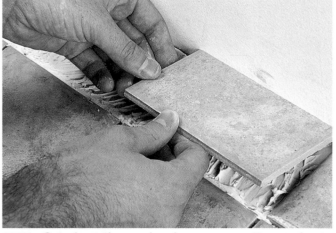

7 *Cut along the mark* using a snap cutter, and set the newly cut edge tile in adhesive.

Cutting Partial Tiles

With all of the full tiles in the main field placed, cut and place all the partial tiles around the room perimeter. If you plan to use cove or trim tiles, you need to allow for the thickness (and a grout joint) against the wall. If the field tiles run to the wall, leave a slight gap between the tiles and wall for expansion.

To measure irregular partial tiles, place a loose tile directly on top of the last full-size tile. Place another loose tile on top of that one, and move it against the wall. Using the back edge of that top tile as a guide, draw a line on the surface of the loose tile below. That's the one you cut. This off-set method of measuring is also handy if you need to trim L-shaped tiles at corners. Remember to allow for the grout joint.

Joint Spacing

To ensure even spacing for grout joints, some tiles have small spacing nubs molded into the edges. When you set two of these tiles together, the nubs match up and create a gap for grout. If the tiles you are using do not have nubs, use molded plastic spacers in the gaps.

These cross-shaped spacers are available in many sizes (generally from $\frac{1}{32}$ inch to $\frac{1}{2}$ inch), so you can use them on small tiles with narrow

Installing Partial Tiles and Finishing the Job

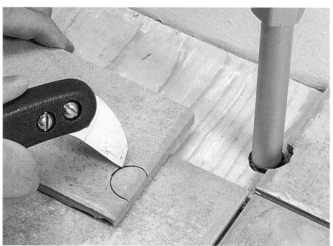

1 *Use a scoring tool* to scratch the surface of the tile before cutting out obstructions with nippers.

2 *Slowly nip up to the score line* with tile nippers. File the edge smooth if it will show.

5 *Pull the grout* diagonally across the seams between tiles using a rubber float.

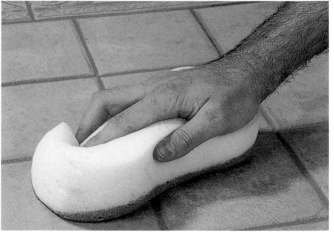

6 *Dampen a sponge,* and clean the haze from the face of the tiles. You'll need more than one pass.

grout lines and on large tiles with thick grout lines. Follow the tile manufacturer's recommendations as to size and type to use. Some can be set flat, left in place, and grouted over.

Finishing Tiles

Before you grout the tile joints, the adhesive needs to cure. That could take 24 to 48 hours. Check the manufacturer's recommendations to be sure. To apply grout, the typical procedure is to spread a liberal amount across the tile surface, working on a diagonal to the joints with a rubber float or squeegee. With repeated passes you gradually force grout into the joints and compact it.

Do not use grout to fill the space between the last row of floor tiles and the wall. Instead, use flexible silicone caulk to allow for expansion and contraction between the different materials.

As soon as the grout becomes firm, use a wet sponge to wipe off excess grout from the tile surface. On most jobs it takes several passes (rinsing the sponge frequently and changing the water, too) before the final grout haze is removed. You may be able to leave the grout joints flush, or nearly flush, just by working the seams with your trowel. In wet areas (mainly bathrooms) you can retard surface mildew and protect grout seams by adding a sealer such as liquid silicone.

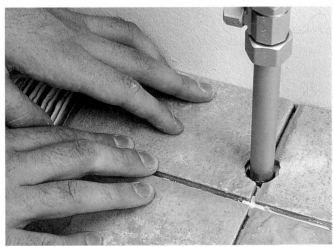

3 *Fit the trimmed tile* into place on adhesive. Use caulk instead of grout around obstructions.

4 *Slowly add water* to mix grout from dry ingredients. It comes in different colors, or you can add coloring.

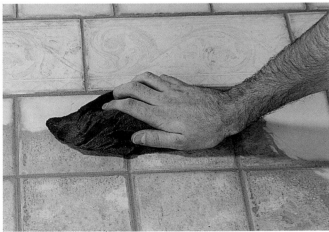

7 *After several passes* with the sponge, use a clean damp cloth to finish the job.

8 *Apply a clear silicone sealer* in wet areas such as kitchens and baths to preserve the grout.

CHAPTER 8 Tile

Setting Wall Tile

Installing wall tile involves the same general procedures described for installing floor tile earlier in this chapter. But you lay wall tiles from the lowest point up, so the tiles and spacers can support the next course. Most adhesives used for wall tile are formulated to hold the tiles in place while still wet. These include thinset latex portland cement and organic mastic adhesives.

On simple wall installations, you can establish a center grid for field tiles by measuring and then snapping chalk guidelines. If the end tiles will be less than one-half tile wide, move the vertical guideline a distance of one-half tile to the right or left of the centerline. This will result in wider partial tiles at each end.

You also need to establish a level horizontal baseline to ensure that the first row—and all rows above it—will be level.

The Tiling Sequence

You have two basic options for laying field tile on a wall. You can build up the tiles from the center of the wall in a pyramid shape or lay the length of the bottom row and work from one corner. If you use trim tiles at floor level, typically you set all of them first and then fill in above them with field tiles. Install trim pieces for inside and outside corners just ahead of the whole field tiles, filling in with cut pieces as needed.

After spreading the adhesive, press each tile into place with a slight twisting motion to embed it. Frequently check the alignment using a level. Also check across the wall surface with a straightedge to make sure all tiles are seated the same way. If you find one that's raised, apply more pressure before the adhesive sets up. If a tile is embedded below the others, pry it out, butter the back with additional adhesive, and reset it flush.

Use a float to spread grout into the joints. Work the float with diagonal sweeps to force the material thoroughly into the seams. However, where the wall tile meets the floor you should use a flexible caulk to fill the joint and to avoid eventual cracking at this intersection of different materials.

Installing and Finishing Wall Tile

TOOLS
- Notched trowel
- Hammer
- 4-foot level
- Pencil
- Bucket
- Sponges and rags
- Float
- Grout bag (optional)

MATERIALS
- Grout mix
- Water
- Grout sealer
- Nails
- Spacers
- Duct tape
- Adhesive
- Tile

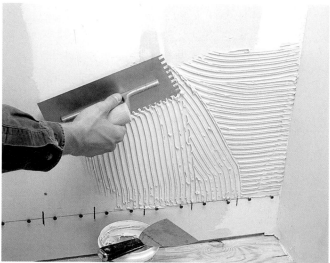

3 *Prepare to set the field tiles* above the nails by spreading adhesive with a notched trowel.

6 *When the main field is secure*, pull the nails and set the bottom row. Tape prevents sagging.

1 *Establish a level baseline* for the field tiles, measuring up from the high point of the floor.

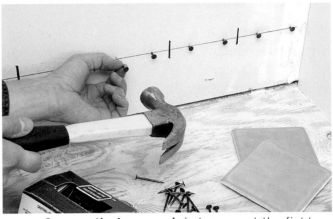

2 *One practical approach* is to support the field tiles and prevent sagging with pairs of nails.

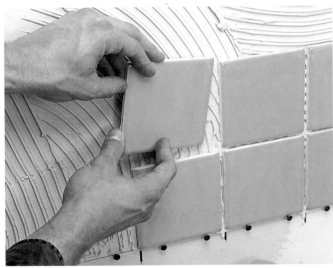

4 *Set the field tiles* into the adhesive bed with light pressure, working up to a guideline.

5 *Use spacers in grout seams* to maintain alignment and transfer weight down to the first row.

7 *When the tiles are fixed* (generally in 24 hours), spread grout into the seams with a float.

8 *Grout leaves a haze.* You need several passes with a clean, damp sponge to clear it away.

CHAPTER 8 **Tile**

Maintenance and Repair

For day-to-day cleaning, simply wipe down tile with warm water and a sponge. On floors, regular sweeping or vacuuming should prevent dirt and grit from scratching the tile surface and grinding into grout joints.

For stubborn stains, try a strong solution of soap-free, all-purpose cleaner or a commercial tile cleaner. Don't use acid-based cleaners because they can attack grout. Always rinse thoroughly with clean water. After cleaning unglazed tiles, reseal them.

If you really need to scour the surface, use a woven-plastic pot scrubber rather than steel wool, which sheds flecks of metal that leave rust stains in grout joints. Avoid using soap-based detergents because they generally dull the tile surface. Remember not to mix different types of cleaners, and never mix ammonia with bleach or products that contain it. That combination can produce lethal fumes.

Fixing Common Problems

In most households there are two common cleaning problems: mildew on tile grout, and a buildup of soap scum that's sometimes com-

Cleaning Old Grout

TOOLS
- Grout brush or toothbrush
- Rubber gloves
- Safety glasses
- Sealer applicator

MATERIALS
- Bleach or grout cleaner
- Grout sealer

1 *Pour grout cleaner or straight bleach* onto mildew-stained grout. Test it in a small section first.

2 *On stubborn stains* let the agent sit for a few minutes. Brushing will help dislodge stains.

3 *After the grout dries,* apply a clear sealer to reduce future staining and cleaning.

bined with hard-water scale. To clean grout joints, first rinse the area with water. Then use a toothbrush dipped in household bleach to remove stains. Stubborn stains may respond to a preliminary dose of straight bleach. If the grout is colored, test a spot to make sure the bleach will not cause discoloration. Wear rubber gloves and safety glasses.

To tackle a stain deep in the grout, try a soupy poultice of baking soda and liquid detergent mounded up and left on the spot overnight to draw out the stain. To remove mild soap deposits and hard-water spots, spray the surfaces with an all-purpose, nonabrasive cleaner, and let

it soak in before rinsing. If some deposits remain, mist the area with vinegar, and let it sit for a few minutes before wiping. If all else fails, try a proprietary soap-scum or mineral-deposit remover.

Sealing Grout & Unglazed Tile

You can apply a clear sealer to the grout joints only or to the entire surface, provided you have unglazed tiles. A sealer doesn't eliminate cleaning and periodic repairs, but it does add a measure of protection against stains. The drawback is that you need to reapply the sealer about every two years to maintain protection. Before you can reseal, you'll need to clean thoroughly.

Removing Grout

TOOLS
- Rotary power tool
- Grout-removal attachment
- Grout saw (optional)

1 *Grout-removal attachments* are sold as accessories for rotary tools. Clamp the guide hood over the chuck.

2 *The hood seats the tool* on the tile and keeps the cutter aligned with the grout seam.

3 *Power grout tools* can chew through the entire seam so that new grout can take hold.

Fixing Broken Tiles

Trying to pry a broken tile off the floor or wall can disrupt surrounding tiles. The better approach is to break a damaged tile into pieces that are easy to remove. Start by removing the grout. One way to contain the repair project is to drill a series of small holes in the solid grout bordering the tile. Keep the bit centered, and avoid damaging adjacent tiles as you drill. The holes make it easier to dig out the grout and expose tile edges. You can instead use a small grout saw or the grout-removal tool shown on the previous page. With the grout gone, it's usually easy to pry out the pieces with a screwdriver.

Setting Replacement Tile

Use a wood chisel to scrape and cut away any raised ribs of old adhesive. You don't need to remove all traces, but you do need to make room for a new layer of adhesive. Over drywall, it's difficult to remove a tile without bringing along scraps of paper and some of the underlying gypsum. Patch any holes you make before you apply new adhesive.

Over any surface, work the new tile side-to-side to get a good bond, and leave it centered in the space to maintain even grout seams. Once the adhesive sets (usually overnight), you can add grout to finish the repair.

Replacing Broken Tile

TOOLS
- Power drill-driver
- Masonry bit
- Grout saw (hand or power)
- Utility knife
- Chisel

MATERIALS
- Replacement tile
- Adhesive
- Grout

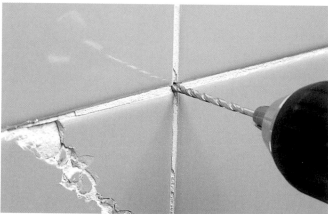

1 **Drill holes** with a masonry bit near the corners of the broken tile to prevent damage to the other tiles.

3 **With the grout removed,** it's easy to pry the remaining tile section off of the wall.

4 **Scrape away** any raised ribs of old adhesive that could prevent the new tile from seating.

Wall tiles in wet areas around baths and sinks should be supported by panels of cement-based backer board.

Smart Tip Cleaning Out Grout

To dig out grout when you need to remove a damaged tile, it helps to first drill out the grout corners (below) with a carbide-tipped masonry bit. The holes isolate the damaged tile and reduce adjacent damage during removal. Small grout saws (bottom) come with both abrasive and toothed blades for removing different kinds of grout.

2 *Dig out the surrounding grout* using a grout saw. Also use a utility knife to slice along the edge.

5 *Spread new tile adhesive* with the end of a notched trowel, and then set the replacement tile.

CHAPTER 8 **Tile**

Ceramic tile can make an elegant, fire-safe covering for a fireplace hearth and face wall. Around a prefabricated fireplace, you can use one type and size of tile, as in this project, or add accent tiles in a row around the opening. In all cases, check local building codes to be sure that you make a fire-safe installation. You'll need to use rugged tile, such as heavy-duty quarry tile, which is resistant to both heat and the impact of an accidentally dropped log. If you are tiling over masonry, use nonflammable heat-resistant mortar, such as a dry-set cement. Do not use organic mastics. Over an existing wood floor, install at least one layer of cement-based backer board. The hearth generally extends at least 16 inches out and 8 inches on each side of the firebox. Before tiling, make sure the hearth (even one you're remodeling) meets code.

Tiling a Hearth

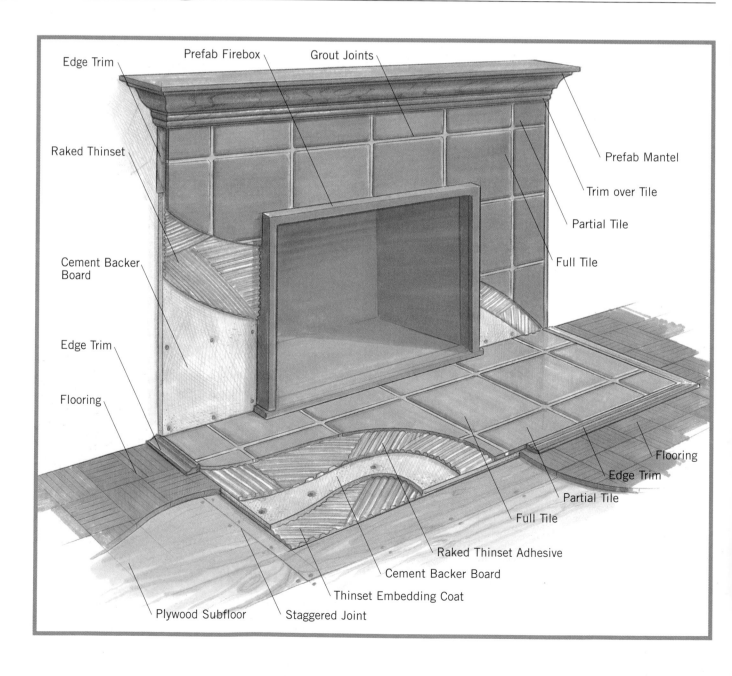

Tile Hearth Installation

TOOLS

- Measuring tape, layout stick
- Chalk-line box
- Notched trowel
- Power drill-driver and screws
- Rafter square and pencil
- Spirit level
- Grout float and sponge
- Caulking gun
- Hammer, nails and nail set
- Miter box and saw

MATERIALS

- Thinset
- Cement-based backer board
- Tile spacers
- Caulk
- Wood for optional trestle
- Tile
- Quarter-round trim
- Trim to surround hearth

SMART JOB TIP

To strengthen a floor for tile and reduce the chances that grout will crack, you can add two layers of backer board set in a bed of thinset mortar. Another option is to double up the supporting floor joists, attaching the extra lumber with construction adhesive and screws.

3 *Snap layout lines* for the tile, and rake out a bed of thinset with the notched edge of your trowel.

1 *Locate the opening midpoint,* and mark the center of the hearth, which should be at least 16 in. deep.

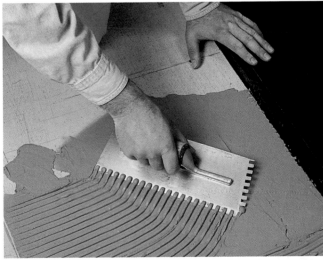

4 *Embed the cut tiles,* full tiles, and edging pieces, allowing even spaces for grout joints.

2 *Score and snap* a sheet of backer board, and screw it down in a bed of thinset mortar.

CHAPTER 8 Tile

WALL PREP FOR WOODSTOVES

You can make a safe woodstove installation by keeping a stove 3 feet or more from the nearest combustible wall. To avoid that inconvenient, space-wasting layout you can buy a stove with a heat dissipating backer plate, and make the installation on a false wall of non-combustible backer board. This detail creates an air baffle against the main house wall.

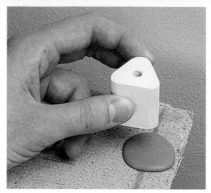

Mortar ceramic spacers to the back of the backer board.

Drill through the spacer, and screw the board to the wall.

5 *Add trim with mitered corners* around the hearth to cover the edges of the tile and backer board.

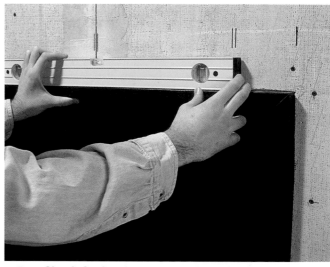

6 *Check for level* across the fireplace lip on a prefab unit, or across the lintel of a masonry opening.

9 *Use spacers* to maintain alignment and transfer the weight of the tiles down to the fireplace lip.

10 *Grout the joints* once the tile has securely set. Clean off dried grout haze with a damp sponge.

TRIMMING AT STOVEPIPES

Ceramic tile is a good choice for woodstove hearths and walls as well as fireplaces, as long as it is set on a fire-safe substrate mounted off the main wall and according to local codes. Set wall tiles in a bed of thinset raked out with a notched trowel, maintaining grout joint lines with spacers. You need to make cuts to add accents and fit tiles around stovepipes.

Use a nipper to trim tiles within about ½ in. of the stovepipe.

A stovepipe trim ring will cover rough-cut edges and open seams.

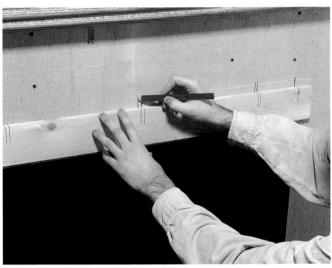

7 *Use a layout stick* with grout spaces to mark full tiles and equal-cut tiles on each side of the opening.

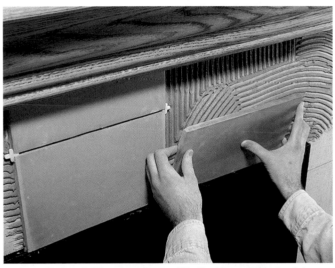

8 *Set cut tiles* to align with the hearth layout in a bed of thinset raked out over the substrate.

11 *Trim the edges with wood,* only if clearances from the fireplace opening comply with local codes.

12 *Fill the expansion joint* between face and hearth tiles with a bead of flexible caulking.

CHAPTER 8 Tile

A plain concrete slab may serve well enough as a landing or small patio to keep you up off the grass and soil as you enter and leave the house. But it's not very attractive. This project builds on an existing slab, adding a decorative and sturdy layer of tile. You could also use pavers or other masonry units rated for exterior installation. If your slab is sound, you can jump into this project at Step 10, where you start laying tile. If your slab is only a few inches thick, cracked, or sunken, start from scratch. Here you'll see how to form around the existing concrete and pour a secondary slab reinforced with wire mesh. One concern is the joint against the house wall. To prevent cracking and still make the seam weatherproof, you need to pack foam backer rod into the joint and finish the surface with flexible, exterior-grade caulk.

Patio Entry

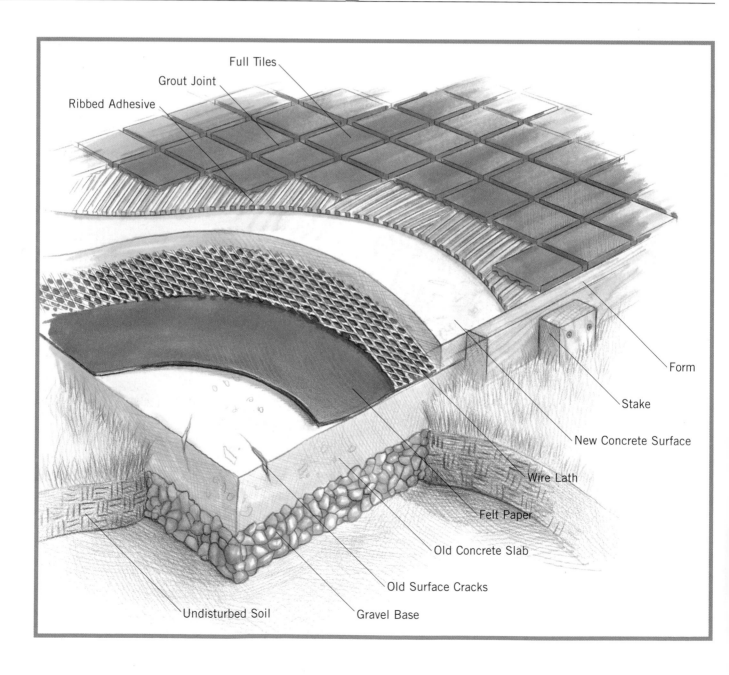

Full Tiles
Grout Joint
Ribbed Adhesive
Form
Stake
New Concrete Surface
Wire Lath
Felt Paper
Old Concrete Slab
Old Surface Cracks
Undisturbed Soil
Gravel Base

Patio Entry Installation

TOOLS
- Power drill and caulking gun
- Mortar hoe and metal float
- Sponge and bucket
- Chalk-line box
- Snap cutter or tile saw
- Notched trowel
- Grout float or squeegee
- Sponge mop (for applying sealer)
- Rubber mallet
- Putty knife

MATERIALS
- Screws
- Builder's felt paper
- Wire lath
- Lumber for form and screeds
- Concrete
- Tile, adhesive, and spacers
- Grout, caulk, and sealer
- Plastic sheeting
- Foam backer rod

SMART JOB TIP
To create a slight slope that encourages surface runoff, simply set a piece of gravel under the midpoint of the center screed board. As you pour and screed the upper slab, this will build a gradual and basically unnoticeable slope into the patio surface.

1 *Verify the condition* of your existing slab. If necessary, build a form to contain a new surface pour.

2 *Cover the old surface* with 30-lb. felt paper to prevent cracks from continuing into the new pour.

3 *Roll sheets of wire lath* onto the builder's felt. This will reinforce the new concrete pour.

4 *Screw intermediate screeds* to the form on large slabs where forms can't support all screeding.

CHAPTER 8 Tile

PIPE SCREEDS

Some slabs are too large or shaped too irregularly to screed with a single board. In this case you can install intermediate screeds to control surfacing. One option is to use wood screeds (shown in step 6 below). Another is to use lengths of pipe supported on stakes. After you screed the surface you need to remove the pipes and then fill and smooth the narrow troughs.

Drive stakes into the gravel to support the temporary screed pipes.

Drive pairs of nails to hold the pipes in place on the stakes.

5 **Pour concrete into the form**; spread it into the corners; and add more to reach the tops of the forms.

6 **Screed excess concrete** off the pour by moving a straight 2x4 back and forth along the screeds.

9 **Add concrete to fill the recesses** left by the screed boards, and finish with a float.

10 **Snap lines** to lay out the tile after the slab has cured. Always make a dry layout first.

CONCRETE SURFACE PROBLEMS

Spalling can leave an older slab looking chipped and pitted. In some cases the surface may be missing large chunks that need to be filled before you can lay tile. To prevent spalling in a new pour, be sure to mix dry ingredients thoroughly before adding water. When finishing, do not overfloat the surface. That can leave a thin, watery layer of cement.

Spalling leaves a concrete surface looking chipped and pitted.

7 *Finish the surface of the slab using a metal float, moving it side to side across the surface.*

8 *Unfasten the intermediate screeds, and carefully lift them from the surface of the pour.*

11 *Spread adhesive up to layout lines in a small area of the field using a notched trowel.*

12 *Embed the field tiles; check the surface for flatness; and insert plastic spacers in the seams.*

CUTTING TILE

To use a snap cutter, position the tile against the stop at the head of the tool and draw the scoring wheel across the surface. After making the scoring stroke, press down to split the tile along the score line. To use a wet saw, hold the tile on the cutting table and feed the work into the blade. A circulating system feeds water onto the cutting area to lubricate the blade.

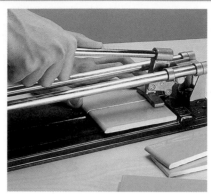

A snap cutter makes a square score line and snaps the tile.

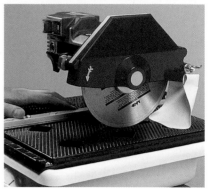

A power wet saw cuts tile using a water-lubricated masonry blade.

13 *Measure the sizes* of the edge pieces, and trim full tiles to size with a snap cutter.

14 *Place the edge tiles,* and continue installing field tiles. A rubber mallet can help to level them.

17 *Cover the backer rod* with exterior-grade caulk to prevent cracking between dissimiliar materials.

18 *Grout the tile* by working the mix on the diagonal to the seams with a rubber float or squeegee.

SPACING TILE

To maintain even spaces that result in uniform grout lines, the surest approach is to insert small plastic spacers between tiles. (You can also use a story pole marked for tiles and grout lines.) Suppliers sell several different sizes of spacers. You usually remove them before grouting. But check with the tile manufacturer because some spacers can be left under grout.

Keep tiles aligned and grout joints even by using plastic spacers.

15 **Cover the tile** with plastic sheeting to protect the installation and help the adhesive cure.

16 **Push foam backer rod** into the seam between the slab and the house and any control joints.

19 **Remove the grout haze** using a damp sponge. Clean the sponge regularly in a bucket of water.

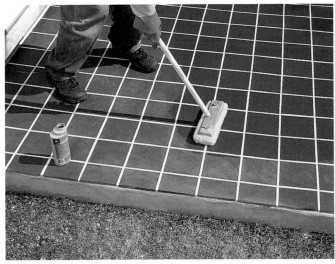

20 **Finish by applying a clear tile sealer** to the entire surface with a sponge mop.

Tile Gallery

Tile is often the material of choice in kitchens and baths. The great variety of colors and finishes allows you to create an almost limitless number of patterns and color combinations. Tile also works in entryways, on patios, and anywhere you need a material that can withstand the elements.

Weather-resistant *forms of tile can provide durable, low-maintenance surfaces for patios and porches (opposite).*

Textured tile *with matching edge pieces (above left) offers character while unifying large countertops.*

Unique walls *can be made by using tiles of contrasting colors. A random color pattern livens up a kitchen (above right).*

Because of its durability, *ceramic tile is commonly the material of choice in kitchens and bathrooms (left).*

Tile is available in a number of styles and textures. A rough, stone-like surface brings an earthy feel to a kitchen floor (opposite).

◥

A checkered tile wall and backsplash open up a kitchen (top left) and creates a contrast to the stainless-steel range.

◥

Create patterns with tiles to draw attention to a space (top right).

◥

To give a room a truly unique look, create a floor using custom tiles (above right).

◥

Tile is a popular choice in bathroom construction. A tan motif (left) is both understated and elegant.

Resource Guide

American Institute of Architects (AIA) *offers a Web site with up-to-date news, an event calendar, job postings, and other information. The main purpose of the AIA's Web site is to help professionals in the architectural business.*
www.aiaonline.com

Ceramic Tile Institute of America, Inc., *supports the expanded use of ceramic tile. Its Web site is a good source of information about tiling.*
12061 W. Jefferson Blvd.
Culver City, CA 90230
Phone: 310-574-7800
www.ctioa.org

American Nursery and Landscaping Association (ANLA) *offers educational seminars and other services to its members.*
1000 Vermont Ave., NW
Ste. 300
Washington, DC 20015
Phone: 202-789-2900
www.anla.org

Concrete Foundations Association *provides educational materials to contractors in 26 states and Canada.*
107 First St. W
P.O. Box 204
Mount Vernon, IA 52314
Phone: 319-895-6940
www.cfawalls.org

The Brick Industry Association *promotes manufacturers' and distributors' interests and helps designers and architects.*
11490 Commerce Park Dr.
Reston, VA 20191
Phone: 703-620-0010
Fax: 703-620-3928
www.bia.org

Concrete Masonry Promotions Council (CMPC) *educates design professionals and the public about the advantages of concrete masonry systems.*
2212 Youngs Dr.
Haymarket, VA 20169
Phone: 703-753-8644
www.cmpconline.org

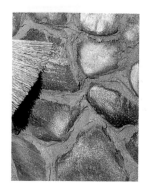

Cast Stone Institute *is a nonprofit trade organization that aims to improve the quality of cast stone.*
10 West Kimball St.
Winder, Georgia 30680
Phone: 770-868-5909
Fax: 770-868-5910
www.caststone.org

Cultured Stone Corporation *is a division of Owens Corning that produces manufactured stone veneers for the home.*
P.O. Box 270
Napa, CA 94559
Phone: 800-255-1727
Fax: 707-255-5572
www.culturedstone.com

EIFS Alliance *provides consumers and manufacturers with general information about exterior insulation finishing systems, such as news updates, articles, and events. The EIFS Alliance can be contacted through its Web site.*
www.eifsalliance.com

International Code Council (ICC) *establishes and promotes modern building codes for consumers and professionals.*
5203 Leesburg Pike, Ste. 600
Falls Church, VA 22041
Phone: 888-422-7233
Fax: 703-379-1546
www.iccsafe.org

Eldorado Stone Corporation *manufactures stone veneer that is easy to install and weatherproof. It can be applied without a special foundation.*
P.O. Box 489
Carnation, WA 98014
Phone: 800-925-1491
www.eldoradostone.com

Interlocking Concrete Pavement Institute (ICPI) *aims to increase product awareness and use in the concrete pavement industry.*
14441 St. NW, Ste. 700
Washington, DC 20005
Phone: 202-712-9036
Fax: 202-408-0285
www.icpi.org

The Hearth, Patio, and Barbecue Association (HPBA) *promotes the hearth products industry.*
1601 N. Kent St., Ste. 1001
Arlington, VA 22209
Phone: 703-522-0086
Fax: 703-522-0548
www.hpba.org

The International Conference of Building Officials (ICBO) *provides safety in the building environment by promoting construction codes and standards.*
5360 Workman Mill Rd.
Whittier, CA 90601
Phone: 800-284-4406
www.icbo.org

Hitachi Power Tools *makes hand-held, heavy-duty power tools for wood, metal, and concrete that are high speed and have a long life span.*
3950 Steve Reynolds Blvd.
Norcross, GA 30093
Phone: 800-448-2244
www.hitachi.com

The International Masonry Institute *improves market promotion in the masonry industry.*
The James Brice House
42 East St.
Annapolis, MD 21401
Phone: 410-280-1305
Fax: 301-261-2855
www.imiweb.org

Resource Guide

Marble Institute of America *promotes the use and expansion of natural stone as a building material.*
28901 Clemens Rd., Ste. 100
Westlake, OH 44145
Phone: 440-250-9222
Fax: 440-250-9223
www.marble-institute.com

The Masonry Society *is an international group interested in the science, art, and advancement of masonry.*
3970 Broadway, Ste. 201-D
Boulder, CO 80304
Phone: 303-939-9700
Fax: 303-541-9215
www.masonrysociety.org

Marshalltown Trowel Company *sells a variety of quality tools to homeowners and masonry professionals.*
104 South 8th Ave.
Marshalltown, IA 50158
Phone: 641-753-5999
Fax: 641-753-6341
www.marshalltown.com

MK Diamond Products, Inc., *manufactures tools such as coring bits and drills, tile, concrete, diamond blades, and cutting saws for contractors.*
1315 Storm Pkwy.
Torrence, CA 90501
Phone: 800-845-3729
www.mkdiamond.com

The Mason Contractors Association of America (MCAA) *represents mason contractors' needs and promotes the use of masonry through programs.*
33 S. Roselle Rd.
Schaumberg, IL 60193
Phone: 800-536-2225
www.masonryshowcase.com

The National Association of Home Builders (NAHB) Research Center *offers information about housing technology.*
400 Prince George's Blvd.
Upper Marlboro, MD 20774
Phone: 800-638-8556
Fax: 301-430-6180
www.nahbrc.org

Masonry Advisory Council *provides information regarding masonry design and practices, including a directory and a technical library.*
1480 Renaissance Dr. #401
Park Ridge, IL 60068
Phone: 847-297-6704
www.maconline.org

National Concrete Masonry Association *supports programs that promote the safety of construction projects.*
13750 Sunrise Valley Dr.
Herndon, VA 20171
Phone: 703-713-1900
Fax: 703-713-1910
www.ncma.org

National Stone, Sand, and Gravel Association (NSSGA) *promotes and supports the aggregate industry.*
1605 King St.
Alexandria, VA 22314
Phone: 703-525-8788
Fax: 703-525-7782
www.nssga.org

Stone-X *is a directory that promotes the use of natural stone for the construction industry. Stone-X aims at improving business by sharing expertise, knowledge, and experience. Stone-X can be contacted through its Web site.*
www.stone-x.com

Portland Cement Association *provides handbooks, resources, and research reports to improve the quality of construction.*
5420 Old Orchard Rd.
Skokie, IL 60077
Phone: 847-966-6200
Fax: 847-966-8389
www.portcement.org

Stuc-O-Flex International, Inc., *provides reasonably priced EIFS finishes and exterior insulations for home renovations, construction, and repairs.*
17639 NE 67th Ct.
Redmond, WA 98052
Phone: 800-305-1045
www.stuc-o-flex.com

Prosoco, Inc., *is a custom formulator of protective treatments and cleaners that improve masonry and concrete.*
3741 Greenway Cir.
Lawrence, KS 66046
Phone: 800-255-4255
Fax: 785-830-9797
www.prosoco.com

The Tile Council of America *provides literature and technical assistance for tile installation and maintenance.*
100 Clemson Research Blvd.
Anderson, SC 29625
Phone: 864-646-8453
Fax: 864-646-2821
www.tileusa.com

Stoneinfo.com, *a division of KD Resources, is a Web site that offers valuable information to construction professionals.*
8711 E. Pinnacle Peak Rd.
Scottsdale, AZ 85255
Phone: 480-502-5354
Fax: 781-394-0599
www.stoneinfo.com

Unilock *manufactures pavers and retaining wall building products. They have over 350 dealers in the United States and Canada.*
51 International Blvd.
Brewster, NY 10509
Phone: 800-864-5625
www.unilock.com

Glossary

Actual dimensions The measured dimensions of a masonry unit as opposed to its nominal size that includes mortar joints.

Aggregate Crushed stone, gravel, or other material added to cement to make concrete. Gravel and crushed stone are considered course aggregate; sand is considered fine aggregate.

Brick Clay that is molded to shape and fired at very high temperatures in a large kiln or oven. The color of the natural clay determines the color of the brick.

Brick set Hardened masonry chisel, often with a wide cutting edge, used to score and cut masonry.

Broom Finish The texture created when a concrete surface is brushed with a stiff broom before it hardens.

Building Bricks Also called common bricks, these bricks are rough in appearance but are structurally sound. Some building bricks have slight deformations.

Buttering Placing mortar on a masonry unit with a trowel before setting the unit in place.

Concave Joint A masonry joint that is recessed and formed in mortar. A curved steel jointing tool is used to make a concave joint.

Concrete A semifluid mixture of portland cement, sand, gravel or crushed stone, and water.

Concrete Block A masonry unit that consists of an outside shell with a hollow center that is divided by two or three vertical webs.

Concrete Pavers Commonly used for driveways, patios, and sidewalks; available in many shapes and sizes.

Control Joints Surface joints that allow concrete stress cracks to form in straight lines at planned locations.

Curing Providing proper moisture, typically to a concrete slab, so that the mix reaches maximum strength without cracking or shrinking.

Darby A long-handled tool used for smoothing the surface of a concrete slab.

Edging Joints The rounded-over edges of a pour that are resistant to cracking and chipping.

Face Brick A type of brick used when a consistent appearance is required. A batch of face brick will be uniform in color, size, texture, and structure.

Firebrick A brick made of a special clay and baked at an extremely high temperature to make the unit resistant to heat.

Flagstone Patterning Carving a design onto the surface of concrete to make a pattern.

Flashing Masonry flashing can be made of metal, rubberized asphalt sheet membranes, or other materials. It controls moisture in masonry walls by keeping the top of a wall dry.

Floating The process of smoothing the surface of a concrete pour with a float made of steel, aluminum, magnesium, or wood. This action raises fine particles and water to the surface.

Footing Concrete used to support masonry walls, typically twice the width of the wall and at least as thick; poured below the frost line to avoid damage from frost heave.

Formwork The forms, often staked and braced two-by lumber, that contain wet concrete.

Frost Heave Upheaval of the ground resulting from the alternate freezing and thawing of water in soil.

Frost Line The maximum depth to which soil freezes in the winter.

Header The brick position in a wall in which the brick is rotated 90 degrees from the stretcher position so that the end is facing out.

Hydration The process of cement particles in concrete chemically reacting with water and bonding together to make the concrete strong.

Isolation Joints Strips in formwork that separate new concrete from existing adjacent construction and other concrete slabs that might expand and contract differently or experience different soil settlement.

Mortar A mixture of cementitious materials, fine aggregate, and water used to bond bricks and blocks.

Nominal Dimensions The measured dimensions of a masonry unit plus one mortar joint; generally rounding up the actual fractional dimension of the unit.

Pitting the Surface The process of scattering ordinary rock salt evenly over a concrete surface after troweling or brooming, creating a marbleized texture.

Portland Cement A mixture of lime, iron, silica, and alumina fired in a kiln and ground into a fine powder; a main binder ingredient of concrete.

Prepackaged Concrete Mix This mix combines cement, sand, and aggregate in the correct proportions, and requires only water to create fresh concrete.

Ready-Mix Concrete Wet concrete transported from a supplier in a truck ready to pour; generally ordered by the cubic yard.

Reinforcing Mesh Steel wires woven or welded into a grid of 6- or 10-inch squares. The mesh is used primarily to reinforce concrete in flatwork, such as sidewalks, patios, and driveways.

Rowlock A brick laid on its face edge so that the end is visible in the wall.

Sailor A brick generally set standing upright with the face positioned out.

Screeding Moving a straight board, such as a 2x4, back and forth across the tops of forms to smooth and level sand or concrete.

Segregation A condition that results when concrete is overworked—such as when trying to remove air bubbles—and the mix components separate.

Soap A brick that is halved in width.

Soldier A brick that stands upright with the edge facing out.

Split A brick that is halved in height.

Steel Reinforcement Reinforcing mesh or rebar that is used to strengthen concrete and masonry walls; generally placed horizontally (in pairs) in concrete footings and vertically to reinforce block foundation walls.

Stretcher A brick or block that is laid lengthwise in the course. Stretcher blocks have flanges at the ends.

Troweling Finishing the concrete after it has been screeded. This finishing step is mainly for interior concrete without air-entrainment.

Wall Coping The top course of material or masonry units on a masonry wall. Coping a brick wall ties the masonry units together and helps retard water penetration.

Weep Hole A hole in a retaining wall and in most brick veneer walls that allows water to seep through to relieve pressure against the wall. Typically formed by embedding a plastic tube in mortar between joints.

Wythe The vertical section of a wall that is equal to the width of the masonry unit.

Index

Index

Photo Credits

All photography by John Parsekian, unless otherwise noted.

Page 1: Jessie Walker, design: David Haire **page 2:** Walter Chandoha **page 8:** Richard Felber **pages 10–11:** Harpur Garden Library **page 12:** *left* davidduncanlivingston.com; *right* Edifice Photo **page 13:** *top right* davidduncanlivingston.com; *bottom right* Ken Druse; *bottom left* Richard Felber; *top left* Michael Thompson **page 14:** Philip Clayton-Thompson **page 15:** *top right* Jessie Walker; *bottom right* Harpur Garden Library; *bottom left* Stickley Photo•Graphic; *top left* davidduncanlivingston.com **page 16:** *top* Harpur Garden Library; *bottom* davidduncanlivingston.com **page 17:** *top* Richard Felber; *bottom* davidduncanlivingston.com **pages 18–19:** *both* Walter Chandoha **page 20:** Jerry Pavia **page 21:** *top* Positive Images; *bottom right* Harpur Garden Library; *bottom left* Phillip Ennis Photography, design: Armand Benedek & Partners, Ltd. **page 22:** *left* Edifice Photo; *right* Jerry Pavia **page 24:** Michael Thompson, design: Sarah Robertson **page 25:** *top* Camerique/H. Armstrong Roberts; *center* courtesy of Cultured Stone Corporation; *bottom* courtesy of The Brick Industry **page 26:** Tria Giovan **page 27:** *top right* Tony Giammarino/Giammarino & Dworkin; *bottom right* Roger Turk, design Carleen Cafferty; *bottom left* Jerry Pavia, design: Rancho Los Alamitos; *center* D. Logan/Robertstock.com; *top left* Jerry Pavia, design Roger Waynick Garden **page 32:** *top right* courtesy of Ineedparts.com **page 41:** Brian C. Nieves/CH **page 44:** Michael Thompson, design: Marietta O'Byrne **page 45:** *all* Merle Henkenius **pages 46–47:** *bottom sequence:* Merle Henkenius **page 49:** *top* Tim Street-Porter/Beateworks **pages 52–53:** *bottom sequence* Merle Henkenius **page 55:** *top left & top right* Merle Henkenius **pages 56–57:** *top sequence* Merle Henkenius **page 78:** Russ Widstrand **page 79:** *top* Tim Street-Porter/Beateworks; *bottom right* Jerry Pavia; *bottom left* Walter Chandoha **page 80:** Walter Chandoha **page 81:** *top right* Ken Druse; *bottom* Harpur Garden Library; *top left* Richard Felber **page 87:** Tim Street Porter/Beateworks **page 89:** *top* Tim Street Porter/Beateworks **page 90:** davidduncanlivingston.com **page 91:** *all* courtesy of Pittsburgh Corning **page 101:** *all* Merle Henkenius **page 122:** Jessie Walker, architect: Paul Konstant **page 123:** *top right* Walter Chandoha; *bottom* Stickley Photo•Graphic; *top left* Tony Giammarino/Giammarino & Dworkin **pages 124–125:** *top right & bottom right* Richard Felber; *bottom left* Tony Giammarino/Giammarino & Dworkin; *top left* Jessie Walker, architect Gary Frank; *center* Jerry Pavia, design Roger Gainey Garden **page 130:** Jerry Pavia **page 133:** courtesy of Stuc-O-Flex International, Inc. **page 136:** Phillip Ennis Photography, design OPACIC Architects **page 140:** Jerry Pavia **page 150:** Jerry Pavia **page 151:** *top* Jessie Walker, architect: Jim Tharp; *bottom right* Brad Simmons Photography, design: Nottingham Design Associates; *bottom left* Phillip Ennis Photography, design: Nicholas Calder/Calder Interiors **page 152:** *top right* Walter Chandoha; *bottom right* Jessie Walker, builder: Carol Etienne, design: Colette McKerr; *bottom left* Tom Stillo/Omni-Photo Communications; *top left* Positive Images **page 153:** Jessie Walker **page 160:** *left* H. Armstrong Roberts; *right* Jessie Walker **page 161:** *both* Charles Mann **page 162:** Tim Street Porter/Beateworks, architect: Paul Williams **page 165:** *top* Jerry Pavia **page 166:** Positive Images **page 170:** Tria Giovan **page 173:** *bottom left & bottom right* courtesy of Prosoco **page 177:** carolynbates.com **page 196:** Brad Simmons Photography **page 197:** *top* Richard Felber; *bottom right* CH; *bottom left:* Elizabeth Whiting Associates **pages 198–199:** *top right* K. Rice/H. Armstrong Roberts; *bottom right* Jessie Walker; *bottom center* Jessie Walker, architect: Jim Tharp; *bottom left* Jessie Walker; *top left* G. Hampfler/Robertstock.com **page 204:** Jerry Pavia **page 207:** Tim Street-Porter/Beateworks **page 210:** *all* Robert Anderson/CH **page 216:** Phillip Ennis Photography, design: Stuart Narofsky/NZ Design Group **page 236:** Jessie Walker, architect: David Raino Ogden, kitchen cabinets & design: David Smith **page 237:** *top right & bottom right* Tim Street Porter/Beateworks; *center left* Brad Simmons Photography; *top left* Richard Felber **pages 238–239:** *top right* James Chen; *bottom right* Tony Giammarino/Giammarino & Dworkin, design: Maymount Foundation; *bottom left* Russ Widstrand, design: DesignARC, Michael Holliday; *top left* Brad Simmons Photography; *center* K. Rice/Robertstock.com **page 247:** courtesy of Abbate Tile **page 251:** courtesy of American Olean **page 252:** davidduncanlivingston.com **page 263:** Tony Giammarino/Giammarino & Dworkin **page 274:** Richard Felber **page 275:** *top right* Stickley Photo•Graphic; *bottom & top left* davidduncanlivingston.com **pages 276–277:** *top right* Jessie Walker, design: Drury Design; *center right* Jessie Walker; *bottom center* Jessie Walker, architect: David Raino; *left* Tony Giammarino/Giammarino & Dworkin; *top center* Bob Greenspan, stylist: Susan Andrews **back cover:** *top* Jerry Pavia

Metric Conversion

Length

	1 inch	25.4 mm
	1 foot	0.3048 m
	1 yard	0.9144 m
	1 mile	1.61 km

Area

	1 square inch	645 mm²
	1 square foot	0.0929 m²
	1 square yard	0.8361 m²
	1 acre	4046.86 m²
	1 square mile	2.59 km²

Volume

	1 cubic inch	16.3870 cm³
	1 cubic foot	0.03 m³
	1 cubic yard	0.77 m³

Common Lumber Equivalents

Sizes: Metric cross sections are so close to their U.S. sizes, as noted below, that for most purposes they may be considered equivalents.

Dimensional lumber	1 × 2	19 × 38 mm
	1 × 4	19 × 89 mm
	2 × 2	38 × 38 mm
	2 × 4	38 × 89 mm
	2 × 6	38 × 140 mm
	2 × 8	38 × 184 mm
	2 × 10	38 × 235 mm
	2 × 12	38 × 286 mm
Sheet sizes	4 × 8 ft.	1200 × 2400 mm
	4 × 10 ft.	1200 × 3000 mm
Sheet thicknesses	¼ in.	6 mm
	⅜ in.	9 mm
	½ in.	12 mm
	¾ in.	19 mm
Stud/joist spacing	16 in. o.c.	400 mm o.c.
	24 in. o.c.	600 mm o.c.

Capacity

	1 fluid ounce	29.57 mL
	1 pint	473.18 mL
	1 quart	1.14 L
	1 gallon	3.79 L

Temperature

(Celsius = Fahrenheit − 32 × ⅝)

°F	°C
0	−18
10	−12.22
20	−6.67
30	−1.11
32	0
40	4.44
50	10.00
60	15.56
70	21.11
80	26.67
90	32.22
100	37.78

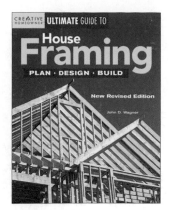
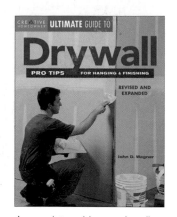

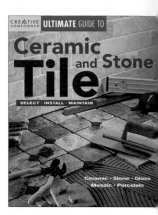
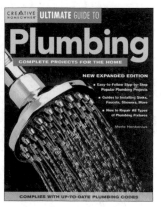
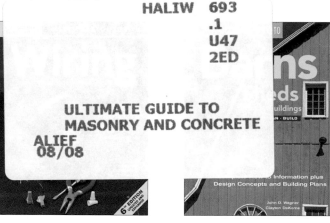

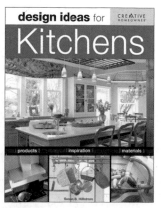